THE VAMPIRE'S BEDSIDE COMPANION

Peter Underwood

First published in 1975

Google Map

peterunderwood.org

Underwood Publishing

DEDICATION

*Dedicated to
the memory of
MONTAGUE
SUMMERS*

*(in the hope that he will forgive me
for revealing some of the secrets of the Vampire Medallion -
and that I shall not regret it..)*

CONTENTS

Title Page
DEDICATION
INTRODUCTION   1
Sighisoara, The Black Chuch and Bran Castle   11
CAN SUCH THINGS BE?   14
VAMPIRES EVERYWHERE   25
PSYCHOANALYSING THE VAMPIRE   45
THE GENESIS OF DRACULA   58
A VAMPIRE TALISMAN   78
VAMPIRES AND HIGHGATE CEMETERY   86
THE HIGHGATE VAMPIRE   94
FOUR NEW VAMPIRE STORIES   150
DOMDANIEL   151
TO CLAIM HIS OWN   191
DIES IRAE   243
MIRROR WITHOUT IMAGE   289
SELECT BIBLIOGRAPHY   316
About The Author   319
Books By This Author   323

INTRODUCTION

On the very day that I begin this book about vampires there is news of a fresh outbreak of inhuman devilry at a cemetery in London that has long had the reputation, not only of being haunted, but also of being the lair of a vampire - and perhaps even the resting-place of a nest of vampires.

In 1974 belief in vampires is still very much alive as this book will show and it may well be that the evidence for the existence of such creatures is terrifyingly convincing. Can such things really be?

Down the ages and from many countries there have been reports of vampirism and acts suggesting the presence of vampires. A hundred years ago the French *savant* Dr A T Pierart (died 1878) stated: 'The facts of vampirism are as well attested by inquiries as are the facts of catalepsy.' As recently as 1970 a news story was published throughout the world concerning a young man named Angri from Medan, North Sumatra, who was in court on a charge (to which he confessed) of sucking the blood of at least two babies and the report pointed out that the man was 'behaving like a vampire' In Djakarta the Associated Press report was headed

'Dracula Arrested' and it was stated that in Sumatra such a practice of blood-sucking is known as 'palasik'. The previous year, in West Pakistan, villagers were reported to be sleeping indoors, in spite of the fierce heat, 'because of vampires'. And in April, 1970, *The Times* reported that an olive grove near Lerici, La Spezia, Italy, was, according to the villagers, repeatedly haunted by a vampire; a figure that appeared in a long black cloak and had a thin pale face with lips drawn back 'in a snarl disclosing two protruding, long and pointed teeth'.

In Italy, in 1952, blood spurted from a corpse that had been buried for thirty years. The body, that of a woman of seventy who had died in February 1920, was exhumed from the cemetery of Aberici di Montemarciano, Ancona, on the Adriatic coast. It was found to be in a 'perfect state of preservation' and blood 'flowed abundantly'. It was only after the piercing of the body that decomposition commenced.

In 1959, in New York, a Puerto Rican youth was arrested for committing assaults and murder at night. He always dressed in a black cloak and referred to himself as 'Dracula'; his utter conviction that he was in reality a vampire resulted in his having no fear whatever of the electric chair which, however, cured all his ills.

In 1974, *This Essex* magazine carried a report that Christina Foyle had a harrowing experience in a haunted room at Beeleigh Abbey that dates back to the twelfth century.

Having spent some time (at Christina Foyle's invitation) in that historic house and in the haunted room myself I do not doubt that strange things happen there.

The haunted room at Beeleigh Abbey. 'Had I been bitten by a vampire? Anyway, I shall never sleep in that room again—ever.'

A few months previously Christina Foyle, recalling that the room (reputedly haunted by the ghost of Sir John Gate who was beheaded on Tower Hill for his involvement with Lady Jane Gray) had not been slept in for something like fifty years, decided to sleep there. All went well until about three o'clock in the morning when everything in the room seemed to be vibrating, and even the water jug spilled over. Christina Foyle awakened to find two tooth marks on her shoulder near the neck and another on one finger.

When he saw the wound on her finger the doctor suggested she ought to go to hospital. This she did and had an operation. She was told that the finger was affected by a germ unknown for over twenty years. 'Had I been living in the old days,' Christina Foyle said, 'people would have said I had been bitten by a vampire. Anyway, I shall never sleep in that room again - ever.'

Less than fifty years ago the Hon. Ralph Shirley studied the subject and came to the conclusion that vampirism was by no means as dead as many people supposed; more likely, he thought, the facts were concealed in the same way as the birth of monsters.

Human nature being what it is, any really eccentric person may give a totally wrong impression to people who do not really know him. Among the interesting personalities who, it has been suggested to me, may have been vampires, is Charles Wade who owned Snowshill, a National Trust property in the Cotswolds, once occupied by Catherine Parr.

Snowshill—does this lovely collection of old buildings have the mark of the vampire?

Charles Wade: a man born out of his time who slept beneath the outstretched wings of a gigantic bat.

There seems to be very little evidence that Charles Wade was a vampire but the fact that he was a man born out of his time; a man who loved period costume, furniture and architecture of a haunting quality; a man who rejected motor cars, electricity and other 'necessities' of modern life; that the darker side of mankind appealed to him (he amassed a truly remarkable and strange collection of macabre objects) and the fact that he had an enormous preserved bat permanently fixed over his bed was enough to convince some people that if he was not a vampire, he was certainly descended from one - which, according to tradition, is the same thing...

The remarkable fascination that vampire lore and legend has for the twentieth-century Westerner is almost vampiric in itself; one person after another becoming captivated with the strange and primitive attributes of the cult, seemingly powerless to release themselves from the unending quest for more and more information, once they have been 'bitten'.

Belief in vampires might be described as an expression of man's inability to accept death as the end of personal existence. This is not the place to consider the interesting fact that belief in vampires often runs parallel with belief in werewolves. Certainly in Germanic legends the magic change brought about by donning a wolf s pelt is emphasised by taking to the woods and living a nocturnal life, a hunter's and a killer's wild and bloody vampiric life. I well recall Robert Eisler's talking to me at length on this point, adding that the word werewolf in Slavonic was *vrkolak* and vampire *upir,* meaning literally, 'he flies away.'

Much of the 'knowledge' of vampires since 1897 has come from Bram Stoker's famous and horrific novel, *Dracula*, which he set in Transylvania. The inaccessibility of the locale of Count Dracula ('the devil' or 'dragon') only added to the mystique of the vampire legend. Now that the area is part of Romania and the country has realised that the associations with vampirism are so firmly ingrained in the popular imagination, the Romanian government is currently restoring a castle, arranging visits to 'Castle Dracula', and exploiting the area as a holiday attraction.

No one knows where it all began but the Greeks, the Romans and the ancient Egyptians all knew about vampires and the Assyrians and the Babylonians believed in them. What has been described as a representation of a female vampire in the act of copulation with a male victim forms the 'decoration' on a prehistoric Persian bowl.

There were hundreds of instances of apparent vampirism in the seventeenth and eighteenth centuries, especially in Eastern Europe, and not a few in the nineteenth century, some in England; responsible newspapers of every country (including *The Times*) during the twentieth century have from time to time published accounts of outbreaks of vampirism without comment or undue emphasis in addition to reports of people who have been regarded as vampires.

Rumours, reports and remarks of such vampire activity have long become associated in the public mind with the vampire of fiction: Thomas Peckett Preskett's

Varney the Vampire (1847); Sheridan Le Fanu's *Carmilla* (1872); Guy de Maupassant's *The Horla* (1887); and E F Benson's *Mrs Amworth* (1923) as well as Bram Stoker's immortal story.

In the 1930s, the Hungarian actor Bela Lugosi donned the black cape of 'Count Dracula' (a cape he was to be buried in) and his portrayal of the arch-vampire, although it was by no means the first film based on the book, began the vogue that has continued ever since of films with a vampire theme. Few actors have since surpassed the sardonic and saturnine Lugosi for that particular characterisation, and few films have improved on the supporting cast, settings, or camera-work of the 1931 Universal Pictures production of *Dracula*.

Later Hammer Films, with Christopher Lee as the vampire, helped to keep people aware of the vampire legend and to earn for themselves the Queen's Award to Industry for Export Achievement in 1968 when Christopher Lee was received in audience by the Queen of England!

Unfortunately for the true vampire addict, to whom the supernatural element is essential, the later Elms became more and more occupied with box office demand for sex and gore and the supernatural aspect degenerated to such an extent that Christopher Lee (who is seriously interested in vampires) announced in 1974 that he did not plan to play the vampire count any more.

Even today there are people who claim to be descended

from Dracula. One is Count Alexander Cepesi of Istanbul whose vampiric tendencies have been channelled to benefit his fellow men. Since 1947, according to an article in *Fate* Magazine dated March 1968, he has operated a small blood bank.

Peter Underwood, The Savage Club, London

The Legend of the Seven Golden Vampires (1974): Van Helsing is called upon to deal with local vampires and their attendant zombies

SIGHISOARA, THE BLACK CHUCH AND BRAN CASTLE

Sighisoara, where Vlad the Impaler's father was born

The Black Church at Brasov dating back to the thirteenth century, it got this name after being destroyed by fire in the 18th century

Bran Castle, Muntenia, commonly known as Dracula's Castle

CAN SUCH THINGS BE?

To many people, perhaps to the majority, vampires are creatures of legend and fantasy with no reality, today or at anytime, outside the covers of books. To others who have studied the folklore of many countries and examined the existing reports of apparent vampirism that have appeared over the years and still occasionally appear (in England and on the continent in particular) there would appear to be a considerable amount of evidence that such creatures not only once existed but may still do so. Belief in vampires is by no means dead.

Historical research reveals that from earliest times abnormal creatures - both human and animal - have existed. Such monstrosities form a part of the history of all countries and have become absorbed in traditions and legends, to survive in the folk memory as mythology and to be represented in artistic form in primitive and more recent sculpture, murals, paintings, ballads, culture and literature, to quite a considerable degree.

Superstitious awe inevitably became associated with monstrous beings born, for example, with huge fang-like teeth. The births of such monsters, in common with other seemingly mysterious happenings such as comets, eclipses, plagues and earthquakes, were regarded as portending evil and presaging disaster; often such creatures were considered to indicate divine anger or punishment, a belief that survived until the seventeenth century in Europe. Often, too, such physical deformities were hereditary and the families concerned were regarded as cursed and therefore shunned by most of the community; a situation in which sinister stories and half-true incidents became exaggerated and distorted while the unhappy objects of terror and fear often became almost as cruel and callous as they were believed to be.

In ancient Babylonia monstrous births were so frequent four thousand years ago that prophetic meanings were attributed to various deformities and abnormalities; children born with teeth already cut were believed to foretell that the king would live long into old age and the country would be powerful but the family into which such a child was born would come to ruin.

An example of a malformation with vampire-like attributes is said to have been killed in the neighbourhood of Jerusalem in 1725. A full account of the 'terrible wild monster' is preserved in the British Museum. Suffice it to say here that for many days, in an area fourteen miles from Jerusalem in the vicinity of the Forest Mountain, a strange ravaging of men (and cattle) was discovered. Many bodies were found half eaten. An eye-witness described an assault on a man ahead of him in which the poor victim was almost torn in two by cruel talons and long teeth. The witness fled in terror to the nearest town and related what he had seen.

At length, a regiment of infantry and cavalry located and killed the monster which was thought to have had its origin in a wicked Prince of Tartary who murdered many people by 'opening their veins'. The monstrous 'animal' was known to kill, not for the sake of food, but for the express purpose of drinking the blood of its victims.

A kind of reasoning for the 'existence' of vampires is postulated by the fact that Bram Stoker used real places in Transylvania as settings for his vampire, Count Dracula, and in Stoker's book there are accurate descriptions of these places: the towns of Cluj and Bistrita, the villages of Fundu and Veresti, the Borgo Pass in the Carpathian mountains and, reason some researchers, if these are factual has not the count himself reality?

From this shaky basis a whole folklore of vampirism has flourished with the apparent location of Castle Dracula on the banks of the River Arges and several historical personages vying for place as the original and genuine vampire count.

Mr P Lemnaru, an expert from the Romanian Tourist Ministry, carried out investigations following the discovery, in 1972, near the Borgo Pass, of ruins thought to be those of Castle Dracula, and in 1974, he stated that according to archaeologists the ruins only dated from the eighteenth century and are probably the remains of a fort that once guarded the approach to Bukovina.

Manuscripts have been located, dating from the fifteenth century, which name a Wallachian ruler who seems to have been called by the name Dracula; a prince whose cruel rule was marked with such inhuman, shocking and horrifying outrages that during his lifetime this Dracula was feared to the extent that his name became a byword for cruelty and was used as a warning to wayward children.

Vlad Tepes was known as 'Vlad the Impaler' during his lifetime from his liking, at the slightest provocation, for impaling on iron spikes set into the ground men, women and children who displeased him, and Raymond McNally states that in the fifteenth century Vlad Tepes was called 'Dracula' or 'dracole', although this fact is not known to the present peasants of the region.

Vlad Tepes's method of impalement was refined and torturous. He usually harnessed each of the legs of the victim to a strong horse which applied the necessary pressure once the stake had been carefully introduced into the unfortunate victim's body in such a way that it would not kill instantly. The staked victims were often displayed around the outskirts of the city where the impaled - men, women or children - were exhibited to public gaze for the hours or even days that it took them to die.

Sometimes the impalement (a particularly slow and painful form of death) was from the lower part of the trunk upwards, sometimes from the chest downwards; at other times, even in the case of children, entry was made at the navel. Among Vlad Tepes's other methods of painful death for his enemies or those who had offended him were blinding; slow strangulation; burning alive; cutting off ears, the nose, or in the case of women the breasts; scalping, skinning and boiling alive. At least one proud man had his biretta or hat nailed to his head for refusing to remove it in the presence of Dracula - but another ruler, Ivan the Terrible, inflicted the same punishment on disrespectful diplomats.

On one occasion, when one of Vlad Tepes's own men held his nose at the awful stench of blood during a particularly vicious carnage, the prince immediately ordered the man to be impaled on a high stake, away from the rest of the victims, so that his sensitive nostrils might not be affected by the offensive smell.

No accurate record of the number of impalements is available but one account refers to a visit by Mohammad the Second, Sultan of Turkey from 1430 to 1481, who was by no means a saint himself for following his ferocious capture of Constantinople, Greece and much of the Balkans, he became the terror of Southern Europe. Yet Mohammad the Second is said to have been sickened by the sight of the remains of twenty thousand prisoners rotting on stakes outside 'Dracula's' capital city.

Raymond T McNally and Radu Florescu, in their book *In Search of Dracula*, believe that Castle Dracula was a reconstruction of the Castle of the Arges and the small but impressive ruins, at the source of the River Arges, are all that remain of the castle which Dracula built in the fifteenth century with forced labour: local peasants of Wallachia who were made to work until their clothes fell off their backs.

The castle began to fall into decay two hundred years later and was totally destroyed by earthquakes in 1913 and 1940. Today it is rarely visited by the local inhabitants who believe that the presence of the evil Count Dracula still lingers in the vicinity and certainly the custodian of the ruins always keeps a Bible handy to ward off the spirits of the undead. In view of the eternal interest in the Dracula legend - or reality - the Romanian government's restoration of the castle (or at any rate a castle) will involve inevitable commercialisation but 'Castle Dracula' is likely to become one of the chief tourist attractions in Romania.

Tracing the history of any fifteenth-century character has its difficulties but in the case of Dracula, Prince of Wallachia - or Dracula Voevod - or Kaziklu Bey - or Vlad Tepes - or Wladislaus Drakulya, the task seems well-nigh impossible and the unravelling of legend, fact and fiction is indeed a formidable but fascinating undertaking.

Even his long-accepted evil reputation may not be entirely justified for it appears likely from Hungarian and German sources that a considerably detailed and elaborate plot was organised to discredit the real Dracula and remove him from power; a plot that was in full swing during his lifetime and could well account for many of the published narratives that some researchers have accepted as fact.

Certainly the picture of the wholesale impaler of the Romanian, Hungarian, German and Turkish records is strangely out of character with a man who is also credited with presenting a gold cup for use by all visitors to a fountain in the square at Tirgoviste; a man whose reputation for honesty went so far as to ensure that a foreign merchant was not molested and that his treasure was safe as long as he was in Dracula country.

Against such reports others have to be considered, including those of foreign diplomats such as Nicholas of Modrussa who stated in a report to the Vatican in 1464 that Dracula tortured and massacred forty thousand men and women in one instance; while the Bishop of Erlau maintained that by 1475 Dracula had been responsible for no less than a hundred thousand deaths - a remarkable achievement when it is remembered that the 'real' Count Dracula spent more years in prison than he did on the Wallachian throne. He ruled Wallachia for only six years, from 1456 to 1462 (apart from brief periods in 1448 and 1476) but he was a prisoner of King Mathian in Hungary for twelve years, from 1462 to 1474.

Even in prison Dracula's taste for blood is evident from a Russian account by Ambassador Kurytsin, envoy of the Grand Duke, which tells of the prisoner's persuading his guards to keep him supplied with small animals and birds which he regularly tortured by impaling them on small sticks as he apparently impaled thousands of human beings in his time.

He died not far from the place where his father had been assassinated in battle against the hated Turks, just outside Bucharest, and although accounts of his death vary in detail, he seems to have been isolated and surprised by superior numbers and certainly his head was cut off and sent to the Sultan at Constantinople where, ironically, it was put on open display on the top of a stake.

His body was probably buried in an unmarked grave and tradition has it that it lies on the island of Snagov in the middle of a lake in the heart of the Vlasie Forest, near Bucharest. Excavation on the island revealed an unopened grave containing a deteriorated skeleton, fragments of silk garments, a ring, a crown, a casket covered by a purple shroud and a necklace carved with a serpent or dragon motif, probably part of the insignia of The Order of the Dragon, to which Dracula had belonged.

Appropriately enough there are rumours and talk of Dracula's ghost haunting the still waters of the lonely lake where Dracula's treasure is supposed to have been sunk and where the lost church bell rings on stormy nights...

Vampire legend stretches far back into the past and its effect has shown itself for hundreds of years in different ways. For centuries it was the custom in England to bury the bodies of suicides at crossroads (facing north and south as opposed to Church burial with the body lying in an east and west position) with a stake (preferably of whitethorn) driven through the heart with a single blow, ostensibly to prevent them from rising - a precaution that does not seem to have been entirely effective for there are many reports of haunted crossroads. There was the added precaution that even if the body did rise from its grave, the crossroads would confuse it and it would not know which path to take.

Vampires were known to be active during the hours of darkness and it was considered to be doubly effective therefore if such a creature could be destroyed during the night. A new law in 1823 decreed that the body of a suicide must be buried privately between nine o'clock in the evening and midnight and, significantly, no religious ceremony was permitted. In 1882 that law was removed from the statute book and since then the burial of suicides is a matter for individual arrangement and convenience. Nevertheless the custom of pinning the body of a suicide to the ground continued for some years and after it died out the fear of ghosts and vampires still remained.

Vampirism, it was thought, would most likely result from being a victim of the attentions of an existing vampire but there was also the fear of being buried without proper rites; anyone who had been excommunicated was also likely to become a vampire. Both the latter ideas represent the religious aspect of vampirism as does the fact that vampires were repelled by such items as a crucifix, holy water or a Bible; objects that had presumably been revered in life; yet the idea that vampires are immune from corruption is of post-Christian origin. On the other hand, pagan fear of the dark and everything connected with it is represented by the vampire's liking for darkness, his reduced power and activity during the hours of daylight and his apparent control of the lesser creatures of the night, such as bats and wolves.

Whether or not such things as vampires have existed, or may still exist, records of vampires and vampirism are as old as the world and as recent as yesterday.

A female vampire shows her fangs in *The Satanic Rites of Dracula* (1973)

VAMPIRES EVERYWHERE

Melrose Abbey, that beautiful ruin founded in 1136 and containing, near the east window, the heart of Robert Bruce, once harboured a vampire. He was a monk who flaunted his vows, committed suicide and returned as a vampire. He is said to have pestered in particular a neighbouring abbess who tracked him to his lair and enlisted the help of another monk from Melrose who decapitated the vampire as the monster rose from his coffin one night. With a 'hollow groan' the vampire collapsed and troubled the abbess no more.

Another suicide seems to have produced another vampire at Eastbury, the magnificent but ill-fated Vanbrugh mansion at Tarrant Gunville in Dorset. The house had taken nearly thirty years to build when it was completed in 1753 at a total cost of a hundred and forty thousand pounds; an enormous sum for those days. Yet, for reasons never satisfactorily explained, within a few short years the house was demolished more rapidly than it had been built, leaving only the north wing which remains to this day, a silent testimony to the grandeur that was once the glory of Dorset.

A steward named William Doggett succeeded in borrowing a considerable amount of money from his master. Lord Mel-combe. When repayment was required Doggett was in dire straits for he had parted with the money and there was no hope of paying back what he owed. In desperation Doggett shot himself at Eastbury in a room that had a marble floor and it is said that the stain of his blood could never be removed.

Before long doors opened by themselves, inexplicable footsteps were heard by everyone, and peculiar noises were reported from various parts of the house. In addition Doggett's ghost was seen, his face a mass of blood, and this frightening spectre was reported for many years.

Then, in 1845, during the rebuilding of the church and reorganisation of the churchyard, Doggett's corpse was exhumed. When the coffin was opened the legs of the body were found tied together with yellow ribbon but, more frightening, the body was not in the least decomposed; in fact the face had a rosy complexion, although the course of the bullet that had killed him, from the jaw through the head, was clearly visible. Now the secret was out and after the Vampire' was dealt with in the accepted way, there was no further trouble and there were no more reports of Doggett's bloodstained ghost.

In Ireland there is a persistent legend that a vampire lies buried near Strongbow's Tree at Waterford. Some say the vampire is Strongbow himself, Richard de Clare, Second Earl of Pembroke, who occupied Waterford in 1171; others say it is his wife, Aoife, the daughter of the King of Leinster whom Strongbow succeeded. Aoife is said to have cut her own son in two for showing cowardice: as evidence the truncated effigy in Christchurch Cathedral, Dublin.

The haunted graveyard at Waterford is small and overgrown, a ruined church adds to the macabre atmosphere and for centuries it has been claimed that even after the awful creature had been laid in the customary fashion for vampires, this one still lured young men and girls to the sinister spot on dark nights and many stories can be traced, even today, of curious experiences in the vicinity of Strongbow's Tree.

In Ireland there are many tales of ghostly manifestations at funerals and not a few of them have the stamp of being accounts of vampirism. Take for example the story published nearly two hundred years ago that concerned an Irish priest who died and was buried among his forebears in a graveyard in the hills.

As the funeral cortege was making its way back from the burial a solitary figure was espied, hurriedly approaching the procession. When the figure came nearer the mourners saw that the man was dressed in the clothes of a priest and furthermore those in the first cart saw and recognised the man as the priest they had just buried! The figure passed the cortege, taking no notice of the enquiring glances that noted the pallor of the skin, the piercing eyes, and the exceedingly long white teeth overhanging the full red lips.

The figure walked steadily past the whole procession - and was seen by every mourner - and then disappeared from view round a bend in the road. It was dark by the time the funeral procession arrived back in the village where they stopped at the home of the dead priest's mother who had been too upset by the funeral to attend the burial.

She was found unconscious and on recovery related that she had opened her door half an hour earlier to find herself facing her dead son, as he had been in life, but she particularly remarked upon the excessive length of his white teeth, the coldness of his staring eyes and the death-like pallor of his skin. Fear had swept over her and she remembered nothing more until she had awakened in the arms of her son's mourners on their return from burying him. I have been unable to trace any further reports of appearances of this particular Vampire'.

Hungary, once part of Transylvania, traditional home of vampires, has a long history of the vampire in legend and fact. Indeed the popular pronunciation of the word Vampire' comes from the Hungarian Vimpir'. A leading Hungarian author and doctor of philosophy has informed me that he remembers belief in vampires being very strong in the Hungary of his youth. One graveyard in particular was reputed to harbour a vampire from time immemorial and no one would dream of venturing there at night-time.

Records still exist in Hungary of an outbreak of vampirism that lasted several years. People and animals were attacked at night, most frequently in a thickly wooded area in the vicinity of a cemetery.

The work of a vampire, long suspected by the local inhabitants, now began to be considered seriously by the authorities and they noted the proximity of the graveyard and the majority of the attacks and suspicion began to settle on a man named Huebuer; a tall man with dark, sunken eyes, a stranger to the district, little known to anyone who had been buried in 1725. Eventually the local magistrate bowed to the wishes of the inhabitants and arrangements were made to disinter the body of Huebuer.

At night, by the light ot flickering lamps, the party reached the deserted cemetery, located the grave and began to dig. Soon the coffin was disclosed. It was hoisted to ground level and opened. Inside Huebuer's body looked as though it had been buried only the day before! The corpse had a bloated appearance and there was fresh blood about the lips. It seemed to scream when the inevitable stake was hammered home and in the uncertain light even the eyelids appeared to flicker for a moment.

The body was taken to the nearby crossroads and there, in sight of the gallows, the head was cut off. A huge fire was built, the head and staked body were burned to ashes and the ashes scattered to the four winds. Meanwhile corpses buried near to Huebuer's grave were also disinterred and cremated. Thereafter there were no further outbreaks of vampirism; but of the vampires created by Huebuer we hear nothing.

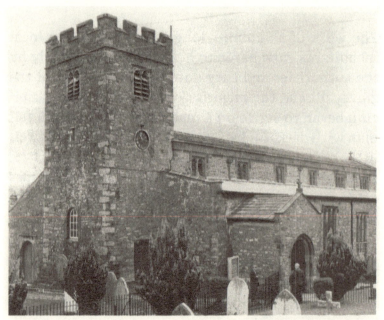

The Church of St Andrew, Dent, Yorkshire. The Hodgson stone is at the foot of the porch, on the right hand side, at ground level

In the vicinity of the church of St Andrew at Dent, a delightful old-world village on the River Dee in Dentdale, Yorkshire, a unique vampire ceremony seems to have been performed to placate the spirit of George Hodgson who 'departed this life' in 1715. A metal stake has been driven deep into the Hodgson memorial stone and through the coffin because the inhabitants were too frightened to open the coffin and drive a stake through the vampire's body. To ensure the efficiency of this extreme action they performed at the same time on the chancel steps a ceremony of sympathetic magic involving transfixing a bat through the heart with a silver pin.

Today what might well be the top of the metal stake that pierced the vampire (or possibly a plug to fill the hole made by the spike) has been moved from its original position to serve as a flagstone outside the church, by the porch entrance. To date no records have been traced describing any terrible outbreak of vampirism that could have led to such extreme and positive action. The present rector tells me that he is familiar with the folklore concerning Hodgson's grave but is unable to say how far it can be substantiated. A local resident tells me she first heard about the Dent vampire nearly fifty years ago - as an undisputed fact.

In the sixteenth century John Weir, a celebrated demonologist and pupil of Agrippa (Heinrich Cornelius Agrippa von Nettesheim 1486 - 1535, the German philosopher and occultist) described an ingenious method of repelling and possibly trapping a vampire.

He advised the consecration of earth taken from the first three spadefuls of soil used at a Christian burial and maintained that if this earth was then trodden under the threshold of the church no vampire could enter and if one was inside it could not get out because it could not cross the consecrated earth to find its grave.

The vampire of 'Croglin Grange' is probably a good example of a factual vampire experience where the site and surrounding details have been embellished to preserve the privacy of a family. There is no doubt that outbreaks of vampirism still occur but they are carefully hushed up: it is, for example, now almost impossible to discover any specific details about the vampire long associated with Glamis Castle, although some stories and in particular one, concerning an ancient fight, certainly suggest the presence of a vampire.

Montague Summers told me that he had talked with Charles Harper who believed the 'Croglin Grange' was in fact Croglin Low Hall; but this place (long a farmhouse) is more than a mile from the rebuilt church where there is ho tomb such as Augustus Hare describes in his reminiscent *Story of My Life.* It has to be remembered that Augustus John Cuthbert Hare (1834 - 1903), a biographer and writer of guide-books, educated at Harrow and Oxford, had distinguished family connections but he was notoriously vague when it came to details. The story bears some of the hallmarks of the romantic fiction of the period but on balance it seems likely that it was based on fact and stripped of extraneous material the story tells of a family (which Hare calls Fisher) who for hundreds of years lived in the curious old house in Cumberland that is the centre of the tale.

The fortunes of the family necessitated their leaving the single-storey 'Croglin Grange' and they obtained as tenants two brothers and a sister who became very popular and well-liked in the district.

After some six months in residence the occupants retired to their respective rooms one hot summer night and the sister fastened her bedroom window but left the shutters open and lay on the bed, propped against the pillows, looking out at the peaceful scene.

She became aware of two lights flickering in and out of the belt of trees separating the lawn from the churchyard and she saw a dark shape emerge from the churchyard and slowly approach the house; a shape which filled her with some uncontrollable horror until she wanted to scream but found that she was unable to do so.

The dark shape turned aside and seemed to be about to go round the house so she jumped out of bed and dashed for the door - when she heard a scratching noise and was horrified to see a 'hideous brown face with flaming eyes' glaring at her through the window.

Rushing back to the comparative safety of the bed,

the terrified young woman tried to console herself to some extent with the knowledge that the bedroom window was fastened, until she noticed the scratching sound had been replaced by a picking or pecking noise and she realised that whatever was outside was unpicking the lead of the window! A few moments later a pane of glass fell into the room. A bony hand appeared through the opening and turned the window latch; the window opened and 'something' stepped into the room.

As the dark figure approached the bed, the terrified occupant still found herself unable to scream for help and then felt a bite in the vicinity of her throat. As her skin was pierced she recovered her voice and her screams brought her brothers rushing to the room but by the time they were inside the bedroom, the 'creature' had escaped through the window.

One brother pursued the intruder in the bright moonlight and he saw the creature disappear with a gigantic stride over the wall at the end of the grounds in the direction of the churchyard. He gave up the chase and returned to his sister whom he found being comforted by his brother. She was bleeding but conscious and expressed the opinion that an escaped lunatic had attacked her.

The wounds in her throat healed without difficulty but on the orders of her doctor, her brothers took her to Switzerland to recover from the shock. There she seemed to forget all about her frightening experience and she wholeheartedly enjoyed the countryside climbing, sketching and collecting mountain flowers. When autumn approached it was she who suggested they return to England where they had leased 'Croglin Grange' for seven years.

Back home she resumed occupation of her previous bedroom but was careful to close the shutters at night although there was still one window-pane at the very top unprotected by shutters. Her brothers occupied a room together nearby and kept loaded pistols by their beds since there had been no reports of any escaped madman being captured.

The autumn and winter passed uneventfully but one night in the following March the sister was awakened by a scratching sound. She looked towards the window and saw the same hideous brown face with glaring eyes looking in at her. She screamed and her brothers rushed into the room, pistols at the ready.

They raced out of the house and saw the mysterious creature running away across the lawn. Both brothers fired at the fleeing figure. One shot at least hit it in the leg and it stumbled for a moment but still succeeded in scrambling over the wall and into the churchyard. There they were just in time to see it disappear into a vault belonging to a long extinct family.

Next day the vault was opened in the presence of all the tenants of the estate. Nearly all the coffins in the vault had been broken open and the contents scattered. One coffin alone remained entire and that one had been recently opened.

Inside lay a brown, shrivelled but intact corpse; the figure that had been seen at the windows of 'Croglin Grange'! There were even the marks of a recent pistol shot in one leg. The corpse was burnt and no more visitations of the Cumberland vampire were reported.

Discussing this interesting account with Montague Summers I recall that he was very much impressed by the resemblance between Charles Harper's drawing of Croglin Low Hall (published in Harper's *Haunted Houses* 1907) and the written description of 'Croglin Grange'. On the point that the family vault in the account had not been located, Summers believed that since the family had long been extinct, the vault could easily have been obliterated. Montague Summers agreed with me that since there was a period of some nine months between the two visits and that 'Croglin Grange' was the only property visited, a suggestion that this particular 'vampire' was in fact a starving monkey from a local travelling circus, seems to be invalidated. In 1974 all my attempts to discover local feelings on the matter from the vicinity of Croglin Low Hall were unsuccessful.

Few Eastern countries have no reports of vampires and a particularly troublesome one was reported from China in 1751. It seems that a courier named Chang Kuei was passing through Liangsiang late at night with urgent despatches when a heavy storm caused him to seek shelter. He made his way to a humble dwelling where the door was opened by a beautiful young girl who welcomed him inside and saw to the stabling of his horse. She dried him, fed him and even extended her hospitality to her bed, with a promise that she would see that he was on his way first thing in the morning.

After a night of great pleasure he awakened to find the sun high in the sky and himself lying stretched out on a tomb in a thicket; his horse tethered to a tree nearby.

By the time he had dressed, made his way out of the thicket, and found the road he had lost in the storm of the previous night, he was hours late in delivering the urgent despatches and when questioned by the authorities on this score, he related the experiences of the night.

Enquiries were made to establish the truth of his story and it was then discovered that a girl who was known to be excessively free with her favours had hanged herself in the wood some years before and that a number of travellers had been detained and entertained in a way similar to the courier.

The courier led the authorities to the tomb where he had awakened and when the tomb was opened the girl's body was found inside, perfectly preserved, plump and firm, with a rosy complexion. The head was cut off and the body burned and thereafter there were no reports of any similar occurrences.

Another vampire flourished in France, it seems, soon after the French Revolution. In appearance he was described as 'an extraordinary-looking man, very tall and thin, with a high, almost pointed, forehead, and protruding teeth.' His name was de Morieve and beneath his suave and kindly exterior there was concealed a cruel disposition - to the extent that in retaliation for the Revolution he took it upon himself to put to death by decapitation all his retainers and workpeople.

Before long he in turn was set upon and killed by peasants of the neighbourhood and no sooner had he been buried than a number of people in the area died suddenly and inexplicably; each with the mark of the vampire on his or her throat. The mysterious deaths fluctuated in numbers over the years but there were a great many (once there were nine in one week) until over seventy years after the death of de Morieve, his grandson succeeded to the estate.

Learning of the appalling cruelty of his grandfather and the continuing deaths, the young de Morieve resolved to see what could be done and after consulting a priest and an expert in occultism, the family vault was opened in the presence of the authorities.

Inside, each coffin was found to be rotted, except that of the old de Moridve; his coffin, after seventy-two years, still looked in excellent condition, sound and strong. When the lid was removed the body inside was found to be fresh in appearance and completely free from decomposition. The face was flushed, there was blood in the heart and chest and the skin was soft and natural to the touch.

Convinced that a vampire had been discovered, the body was removed from its coffin; a stake of whitethorn was driven through the heart - whereupon blood and water gushed forth and the corpse squirmed and groaned. The remains were burned and from that day the mysterious deaths that for so long had plagued the district, ceased. Research in the family archives revealed that the old man had originally come from Persia and it was thought that it was in that country that he had become a vampire.

In the realm of entertainment the vampire theme has gone from strength to strength ever since Bram Stoker published his haunting novel *Dracula* in 1897, a book that has been in print ever since and is as popular today as then. Over the years other writers have produced excellent vampire stories as we have seen and the four tales included in this book show that fine new and original stories on this undying theme are still being produced; stories that will live and add to the 'reality' of the vampire in fiction.

Many writers have been interested in the vampire legend - or reality - and have written vampire stories. Apart from Bram Stoker, Edgar Allan Poe, Guy de Maupassant and E F Benson such writers as Sir Arthur Conan Doyle and Nicolai Gogol have used the vampire motif while in our own time such masters of the macabre as Robert Aickman, Robert Bloch, Ray Bradbury, Simon Raven and Lawrence Durrell have all produced lasting vampire stories. Jacqueline Simpson, author of an excellent work on *The Folklore of Sussex,* has reminded me that there are allusions to vampirism in *Wuthering Heights;* near the end when Heathcliffe is dying.

Although Emily Bronte probably obtained her knowledge of vampires from books and not from English folklore (since she makes Nellie Dean say she has *read* of such beings as vampires) the point is that Nellie, good conventional soul that she is, is so repelled by Heathcliffe's passionate wish for reunion with Cathy that she can only envisage it in gruesome forms; and when she sees the smile on Heathcliffe's face as he lies dead, she can only describe it as wolfish and allude to his sharp and white teeth. There is also the odd detail of Heathcliffe's grazed hand, echoing the gashing of the child-ghost Cathy's wrist in Lockwood's dream at the beginning of the book. If this meant anything literal, it would mean that Cathy was the vampire who had drawn Heathcliffe's blood and so killed him to fetch him to her; and that they were united more perfectly in death than in life.

There have been poems about vampires (one was written by James Clerk Maxwell in 1845) and Goethe, Shelley, Byron, Dryden and Scott all mentioned vampires in their poems and ballads; among paintings depicting vampires one by the influential Norwegian, Edvard Munch (1863 - 1944) who often expressed in his work feelings that seemed to be inspired by a troubled mind. Goya too painted vampire-like creatures.

Vampires have been popular on the stage - there was ap opera with a vampire theme as long ago as 1800 while stage versions of *Dracula* are periodically revived all over the world. The play *Dracula or the Undead* was performed for copyright purposes a few days before the book was published in 1897. Many productions of the play followed and I recall seeing the American version at the old Winter Garden Theatre in London in 1939 with Bernard Jukes as Renfield and Hamilton Deane as Count Dracula.

Actor-manager Hamilton Deane wrote and produced the first real Dracula play in 1924 and he continued to be associated with Dracula in drama for the rest of his life. He had a rare feeling for the vampire count and his remarkable sense of presence gave the play a powerful and exciting ingredient. As one newspaperman said at the time: 'One does not feel easy until he is put out of the way with a stake through his heart'.

The Hamilton Deane play was revised for its Broadway presentation and a then unknown Hungarian actor Bela Lugosi played the title role. It was a part he was to be associated with for the rest of his life and there are those who maintain that towards the end of his life Lugosi really believed that he was the king vampire. At all events he was buried, in accordance with his last request, in his beloved black Dracula cloak.

In films the vampire case has been literally done to death in something like a hundred pictures to date. After such fine films as the silent *Nosferata* in 1922, the early talkie *Dracula* with Lugosi in 1931 and Carl Dreyer's *Vampyr* in 1932, most of the later films were undistinguished and they reached degradation with such efforts as *Old Mother Riley Meets the Vampire*.

Dracula's Daughter in 1936 was an exceptionally good sequel and from the late 1950s up to the present day Christopher Lee and Peter Cushing have given some fine performances in mostly mediocre films although Terence Fisher's *The House of Dracula* (1958) and *Brides of Dracula* (1959) were perhaps representative of Hammer Films at its best.

Peter Cushing as Professor Van Helsing hunts
Count Dracula (Christopher Lee) for the fifth time
in *The Satanic Rites of Dracula* (1973)

I have talked with tall and likeable Christopher Lee and serious investigation of the vampire legend interests him. His remarkable voice was used as narrator and he also took part in a serious film for television, partly filmed in 'Dracula country', called *In Search of Dracula*. After fifteen years the supernatural element receded further and further from vampire films until Christopher Lee became disenchanted with playing the part of Dracula.

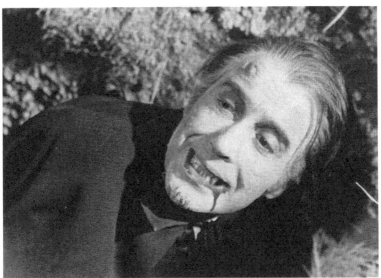

Christopher Lee as Count Dracula

He did however consent to become President of the English Dracula Society, an organisation founded towards the end of 1973 that caters for lovers of the lore and literature of the vampire and his kin. Its activities include visits to places in England associated with Bram Stoker and his creation Dracula. Among these are Whitby where 'Count Dracula' landed in England (disguised as a black dog) and Purfleet where he 'lived' for a time, and where part of Daniel Farson's documentary on vampires for BBC television was filmed in 1974. The English Dracula Society even has plans for an expedition to Transylvania.

In the age of Aquarius the vampire has become a figure of fun to be burlesqued in horror comics but the real thing may, evidence suggests, still be encountered from time to time and if vampires do exist who knows how many there are, or who they are?

Christopher Lee and Joanna Lumley in the Hammer Films Production of Warner Brothers *The Satanic Rites of Dracula* (1973)

PSYCHOANALYSING THE VAMPIRE

The psychologist regards vampirism as a kind of twilight borderland where religious and psychopathological motivations intermingle ambivalently; the death wish conflicting with the desire for immortality; aggression and great cruelty competing with a madly possessive love.

Freud's dictum: 'Morbid dread always signifies repressed sexual wishes' sums up vampirism for the psychologist and he points to the emphasis on guilt, oral activity, the excitement and danger, the variety - one moment blind rage at those who would outwit the vampire and the next sublime pleasure of very primitive origin. Such an explanation: a diseased, hallucinated, psychotic human being could explain a pathological taste for human blood.

European cultures have long encouraged, unconsciously, a love-hate relationship with the dead; a fascination that has resulted in many bizarre and extreme expressions, not only in art, literature, burial customs and monuments but also in differing religions, sects and repressive beliefs.

Vampirism has become a popular term in sexual pathology and as we have seen few countries of the world have escaped reports of such vampirism. Although throughout the rest of this work I use the term in its original and supernatural sense, it may be of value to look briefly at some of the medical examples of 'vampires'.

France had the individual Gilles de Rais in the fifteenth century, a Marshall of France who fought with Joan of Arc, and his lust for blood and necrophilistic tendencies suggest that he was a vampire of sorts. His obsession with alchemy led him to a defrocked priest, Francesco Prelati, who used invocations and the blood of young children in his black magic rituals.

Gilles de Rais discovered that he derived considerable satisfaction from inflicting pain. He drank blood of his victims which satisfied him temporarily and the dismembered bodies of more than fifty children were, it was alleged, found at his home at Machecoul in 1440.

Since the threat by the church of excommunication had considerable effect upon him and he broke down completely and begged forgiveness from the parents of the children he had murdered, he could hardly have been a vampire in the true sense of the term but it may be significant that, after he had been strangled, his body was burned.

In Scotland, Sawney Bean (or Beane) was a bandit and highwayman whose exploits in the middle of the fifteenth century have carved for him a niche in any hall of infamy and more than a few writers have maintained that his insatiable lust for blood suggests that he was in fact a vampire. Living in a remote cave on the coast of Galloway with a woman who seems to have had similar inclinations, he fathered fourteen children. The family lived for twenty-five years by robbing passers-by. The Beans (or Beanes) never ventured into towns or villages; instead they practised incest and the family increased to include eighteen grandsons and fourteen granddaughters. They all existed by cannibalism, pickling the bodies of their victims in sea water and then eating them. For years the existence of the family remained a secret for none of the travellers they attacked escaped and as time passed the region, with its ominous and mysterious high mortality rate, became practically depopulated.

One account tells of a man and his wife being attacked and after the throat of the woman had been cut, Sawney Bean and his family 'fell to sucking her blood' with great relish; the woman's husband escaped, however, and lived to tell the frightful story and to see Sawney Bean and his family executed at Leith in 1435.

The menfolk of the Sawney Bean family bled to death after having their hands and legs chopped off, watched by the women, who were then burnt alive. It is possible to argue that in destroying them a nest of vampires was stamped out.

Even America seems to have had the occasional vampire; or at any rate to have been affected by the vampire legend, for there has long been a widespread belief that as long as the body of a vampire remains intact in the grave, it draws vitality from the remaining members of the family of its victims. In 1874, William Rose of Rhode Island believed that his dead daughter was exercising an evil but very real influence on the rest of his family and possibly other people, to the extent that she was literally draining them of vitality. He dug up his daughter's body and burned the heart.

In Scotland too, within living memory, a man exhumed the body of his daughter and burnt the heart because he thought she was devitalising her remaining brother and sister and making them ill. Whether either daughter was a vampire or not it is certain that the fathers were convinced that, vampire-like, they 'sucked' the life-blood from living people.

According to the London *Daily Express* of 17th April 1925, the body of Fritz Haarmann (executed for twenty-seven murders) was not to be buried until it had been thoroughly examined at Gottingen University and it was stated that the murderer's brain was likely to be removed and preserved at the university. The news item was headed: 'Vampire Brain - Plan to Preserve it for Science.'

Germany after the First World War saw the activities of Fritz Haarmann, a homosexual mass-murderer, who is believed to have killed upwards of fifteen youths, by biting the victims through the throat: a practice that is certainly reminiscent of vampire attack. During the course of his trial it was revealed that the burly Haarmann would hold his victim down with one hand and with a single powerful bite in the throat, kill him. He is also said to have been fond of drinking blood (another vampire characteristic) and on one occasion he was almost caught by a neighbour while he was carrying some human blood in a container. He was known as the 'Hanover Vampire' and is said to have sold the flesh of his victims as meat for human consumption either in the butcher's shop that he ran or through undercover channels as smuggled meat. He was known to be a smuggler among his other virtues.

Haarmann steadfastly denied insanity; he sat impassive and unshakable throughout his trial; maintaining in defence that he was in a state of trance when he attacked people and did not realise what he was doing, nor did he have any control over his actions. The prosecution pointed out that his very method of killing argued premeditation and he was executed by decapitation on 15th April 1925. The Haarmann case used to be referred to by Montague Summers as 'one of the most extraordinary cases of vampirism known.' Of course it all depends on what you mean by vampirism. Summers thought too that it was more than mere coincidence that the mode of execution entailed the severing of the head from the body, long known to be one of the most effective means of destroying a vampire.

I have decided not to deal in detail with comparatively modern cases of so-called 'medical vampirism' such as that of Sergeant Bertrand (known as 'The Vampire') who terrorised the vicinity of Montparnasse in Paris in 1849 when tombs were opened, graves desecrated and bodies violated and mutilated to an appalling degree; but I will review such cases briefly.

Bertrand's activities may have been vampire-like but in reality were necrophilic. At his trial which attracted considerable crowds, the vast majority women of all ages, it was revealed that Bertrand suffered attacks of trance-like states during which 'irresistible impulses' drove him to disinter corpses and violate them. However he was adjudged sane and, probably, because no murder seems to have been attributed to him, he received the somewhat light sentence of imprisonment for one year. Thereafter he disappears from the annals of crime and medical history. Some might claim that his complete disappearance suggests that he was in reality a vampire but there is no real evidence to suppose that he was anything but human, cursed with a curious and obnoxious affliction.

More recently, murderer John George Haigh is often referred to as a 'vampire' because of his obsession with blood. He certainly talked enthusiastically of dreamlike visions that, he claimed, incited him to murder; dreams of forests spouting blood. He maintained too that he was forced to commit the eight murders he claimed to have committed by an uncontrollable urge to drink the blood of his victims. When he killed, he maintained, he usually 'drew off a wineglassful of blood' and drank it 'to refresh' himself.

In his defence, at his trial in 1948, a psychiatrist. Dr Henry Yellowlees, supported the theory that Haigh was paranoiac as a result of his strict upbringing by Plymouth Brethren parents and conflicting involvement as choirboy in a Church of England cathedral; contrasts that resulted in a diabolical development in his character. Dr Yellowlees pointed out that, since, while in custody in Brixton Prison, Haigh had been observed to drink his own urine, he felt it was 'pretty certain' that Haigh had in fact been capable of drinking the blood of his victims. The jury were unimpressed by the guiles of the man a national newspaper had referred to as a 'vampire' long before his trial, and Haigh was duly executed at Wandsworth.

William Seabrook, the adventure writer, related to me his encounter with a beautiful female vampire. The girl was young, an American, pale and thin, quiet, a painter and translator and Seabrook recounts that he often saw her on the beach during a holiday on the Riviera. Once he was swimming and grazed his shoulder. He sat down beside the girl who seemed fascinated by the sight of the blood. She bent close to him, staring at the abrasion and then suddenly jerked forward and fastened her teeth in his shoulder, sucking like a leech. After a moment she slumped back, sobbing, with her face in her hands. When she became quieter she asked Seabrook what she ought to do - have herself locked up, kill herself, or what?

Talking sympathetically to her, Seabrook discovered that she had had similar experiences before and when he suggested that she ought to see a doctor, she had whispered to him the word Vampire'. She had read that such creatures were pale, thin, with red hair and green eyes (which she had) and she believed that she may have been attacked by a vampire while she had been asleep and had thus become a vampire herself.

Seabrook still advised her to see a doctor and to get him to find her a good psychiatrist when she returned to America. She did so but it was too late. Although she never again succumbed to the craze for blood, she was dead within a year, from pernicious anaemia. The red blood cells had been disintegrating and her body had been involved in a struggle to balance itself. Her craving for blood had been physiological but by the time this had been discovered it was too late to save her.

Such cases of 'medical vampirism', interesting as they are, have no place in a study of the vampire of legend who cannot live in the light of day and whose bed is a coffin in his native earth

So what is a vampire? Through more than two thousand years there have been stories of vampires and vampirism. The ancient Romans even dedicated a special day, 13th May, to *Lemures,* the vampire ghosts. In some countries the seventh son of a seventh son will become a vampire, as will a person who has been excommunicated by the established church, or a person born with a caul, or an unbaptised child; elsewhere a suicide will live the life of the undead. The choice is wide and by such criteria many people will be affected; by these standards both my wife and I are doomed to become vampires.

Over the years many individuals, apart from Count Dracula, have acted during their lifetimes in ways that have convinced their contemporaries and suggested to later historians that they might have been vampires; certainly that they have had all the hallmarks of a living vampire. Of such people none is a more prominent candidate than Elizabeth Bathory, the seventeenth century 'Blood Countess of Hungary'.

She was born into an old and wealthy family in 1560 and it is claimed that, necrophilic as well as sadistic, she caused the death of hundreds of young girls; draining them of their blood which she used to bathe in and perhaps drink. After she accidentally drew blood from one of her maids who was combing her hair, some of the girl's blood ran on to the Countess's hand and she thought it made the skin whiter and more youthful-looking.

By the time she was thirty Elizabeth Bathory had already been married for fifteen years and had four children (indeed she had given birth to a bastard at the age of fourteen before her marriage). Now, in 1604, her husband was dead and she acquired a unique and insatiable lust for the blood of young virgins. Over the next ten years Elizabeth's faithful servants provided her with a continual supply of girls, mostly recruited on the pretence of becoming servants at the Castle Csejthe, until it was sajd that several hundred girls were forced to give their blood and eventually, when they had been 'milked' incessantly, their lives to the insatiable countess.

Inevitably one intended victim escaped and notice of the awful events was brought to the attention of the authorities. The castle was raided one winter night in 1610 and Elizabeth Bathory's blood-baths were a thing of the past.

Official documents assert that on gaining entrance to the castle the body of one girl was found, drained of blood but still warm; another was found, just alive, but with her body pierced all over with tiny holes. In the dungeon of the castle an unspecified number of live girls were found incarcerated with only more and more 'milking' to look forward to until they died from loss of blood. As they searched still deeper the investigating authorities located the blood-drained bodies of more than fifty young girls.

The influential countess was imprisoned in her own

castle. She refused to say anything, even to say whether she was guilty or innocent, but she could not save her associates who were tried early in 1611. All were found guilty and were beheaded. Countess Bathory, never formally convicted of any crime, was condemned to life imprisonment in her own castle, but if she thought she had got off lightly she was in for a surprise.

Stonemasons, by order of the authorities, solidified the partitions, walled up the windows, and bricked up the doorways of Countess Bathory's bedroom. She was imprisoned within and fed through a small hole and she remained there, alone with her thoughts, reflections, frustrations and regrets for four years until a guard, peering into the fading, dark and dilapidated room, saw the countess lying face-down on the floor. She was dead and with her death, in a room devoid of mirrors and without a crucifix, Europe saw the last of one of the wickedest women in the world; a woman whose evil deeds were immortalised in a nineteenth-century painting by Istvin Csok entitled, inevitably perhaps, 'The Blood Countess': a picture that depicts the countess leaning back in her raised chair in ecstasy as naked girls are tortured and murdered in her presence.

In more recent times murderers such as John George Haigh as we have seen, have been regarded as members of the vampire clan, mainly because they drank, or claimed they drank the blood of their victims. There was certainly very little, apart from the apparently irresistable urge for blood, to connect Haigh with vampirism. He murdered for gain, pure and simple, and he met his deserved end. Yet he certainly drank blood as an end in itself and without any sexual connotation. When he was a boy, he maintained, his mother would correct him by smacking his hand with the bristles of a hairbrush and when this treatment drew blood, Haigh sucked it and found that he enjoyed the taste; so much so that on at least one occasion he deliberately cut one of his fingers to gratify his growing taste for blood. He said at one stage during his trial: 'It was not their money but their blood that I was after. The thing I am really conscious of is the cup of blood that is constantly before me. I made a small cut, usually on the right side of the neck, and drank the blood for three to five minutes and afterwards I felt better.'

The last sentiment could easily describe the feeling of a true vampire and having now considered briefly the 'medical vampire', the psychotic, the psychopath and the hallucinated, let us turn back to that creature of darkness and mystery, the vampire of fiction and perhaps of fact; the undead, unliving monster who rests in some quiet coffin of ancient earth and whose supernatural element is at once the most frightening and the most attractive of his qualities.

Dr Sir Devendra P Varma is Professor of English at Dalhousie University, Nova Scotia. A renowned authority on Gothic novels - and vampires - he is author of *The Gothic Flame;* editor of the Northanger Set of *Jane Austen Horrid Novels* and he tells me he is currently working on *The Gothic Galaxy,* a study of the minor Gothic novelists. He also wrote a long introduction to the unique three-volume edition of *Varney the Vampire* and his Forewords and Introductions to the Arno Press collection of Gothic Novels have deservedly won warm critical praise. Dr Varma believes in vampires and I am very happy to be able to include a contribution from him in this book: *The Genesis of Dracula: A Re-Visit* is a fascinating account of a visit to Castle Dracula and a new and original theory on the genesis of Bram Stoker's masterpiece.

Countess Dracula (1970); youth and beauty have crumbled away during the wedding service and she has transformed into terrifying old age

THE GENESIS OF DRACULA

A RE-VISIT

by Dr Sir Devendra P Varma

I could a tale unfold whose lightest word
Would harrow up thy soul, freeze thy young blood,
Make thy two eyes, like stars, start from their spheres...
- Shakespeare

Dracula was killed in 1477 while defending Christendom on this side of the Danube, and the Turks carried away his head as a gift to the Sultan of Constantinople, where it was openly exhibited on a stake. Dracula's 'headless body' was buried in Snagov, the island monastery, twenty miles north of Bucharest. The tomb when opened in 1931 by two archaeologists Dinu Rosetti and George Florescu, was found empty. The body was gone! A couple of avenues of conjecture opened up as to what could have happened. One, and by far the most delightfully ghoulish and chilling, is that he turned into a vampire, preying on young men and women. The women, by legend, wear the traditional uniform of a diaphanous nightgown, sometimes in black or sense-titillating pink, but always diaphanous. The second and more prosaic explanation is that the monks at an early date may have burnt his body and scattered the ashes to the winds. Or did he turn into mist and slip away, a talent which vampires alone possess? There have been documented proofs that Dracula the caped count who spent his evenings tippling on the blood of beautiful women, was a real person. He did die and was buried. What happened to his body? Robert Bloch wrote to me:

> How wonderful to learn of your Transylvanian trip! A friend of mine, Alan Dodd, made the pilgrimage about a year or so ago, and sent me a packet of grave-earth; for sentiment's sake, I suppose. He too, commented on the omnipresent mist of evening, and the sense of being under surveillance by the eyes of an unseen presence...
>
> We know *why* the grave is empty, don't we?

Today a strange calm broods over the tranquil setting of the Snagov monastery, but legend has it that shortly after Dracula's burial a violent hurricane swept over the countryside. The monastery built by Dracula's grandfather was uprooted from its very foundations, steeple, bell-tower and all, and submerged into the lake. Superstitious peasants to this day affirm that they have seen Dracula's ghost rise from the waters, and whenever the lake is ruffled by winds, one can hear the muffled sound like tolling of a distant bell. Who knows, perhaps the spirit of Dracula, the great undead, still sojourns there awaiting retribution.

The supernatural terrors and fascination with creatures feasting on human blood, recreated with poetic licence in the fiction of the nineteenth century, have their roots in true events. The fear engendered by the broken bodies of hundreds of pretty maidens, found drained of their blood in the neighbourhood of a Gothic castle in the foothills of the Carpathians in the first decade of the seventeenth century, was real enough. The peasants, wondered, worried and frightened, fixed on Dracula as the villain, saying he had turned into a vampire to prowl the countryside.

Superstition and legend are deeply rooted in this beautifully wild and savage country where the tenor of life has not changed in a thousand years. In the valley of the Carpathians, peasants still hang garlic blossoms on their doors and solemnly warn visitors to the castle: 'Return before nightfall,' and cross themselves. For generations peasants in the surrounding valley have whispered sinister tales of horror enacted within those castle walls. And although they talk about it they rarely muster up courage to visit the ruins. In the prevailing superstitious beliefs, the spirit of Stoker's 'undead hero' still seems to dominate the spot. The nightwatchman guarding the precincts at night clutches an old Bible as if to ward off the evil spirits that hover around. A decade ago the castle's female caretaker gave birth to a demon babe.

Frustrations and mysterious accidents have occurred to several expeditions. In 1969, two American filmmakers ventured there, but were soon rushed to hospital with inexplicable internal bleeding. The atmosphere of the ruins was so eerie, said Professor McNally, that he felt faint and could not bring himself to enter the portals. Professor Florescu came down with a mysterious illness and another member of the team fell into a ravine and broke his hip. A photographer who took the photograph of Castle Dracula died within three days! 'A broken hip and six months in hospital for one of our members' was the fate of another expedition. McNally wonders if it was 'Dracula's way of saying that despite the ruins of his castle, he still rules in some other, unearthly domain?' Were these accidents just coincidences, or bad luck? I grew more curious and wished to explore for myself.

I had seen the antique sixteenth-century oil-painting of Dracula which hangs in Castle Ambras near Innsbruck, Austria. He wears a Hungarian nobleman's tunic, an ermine cape and his Turkish-style fur headdress is richly encrusted with jewels. But it does not hide the cruel and malignant glint of his wide-open green eyes under thick bushy eyebrows; his thin, reddish up-curled lip and black moustache on a pallid shaven face are impressive, and so are the curly locks of jet hair dangling on his wide shoulders. But Stoker's *Dracula* is different: he is a misunderstood anti-hero, a demon-lover, with an aching longing in his heart and the same hypnotic gleam of the eye. He too has vivid red lips, and a mien full of 'lonesome sadness'. The concept of the undead subsisting on the life-blood of its victims remains a voluptuous idea, for what an experience it must be to be embraced by a female vampire? Professor Walter Storkie of California, an authority on vampire lore in Hungary, Romania, Yugoslavia and Greece, had once written to me:

> We certainly have the subject of Vampires in common, for I too, have been interested in them for many years since my first visit to Hungary in 1929 where I had a vampire experience.

In the spirit-haunted wild Carpathian mountains still stand, gaunt and lonely, the ruins of Castle Dracula, as if beckoning from the realm of death and oblivion through the dark passage of centuries. There is something grandiose and plaintive in those sinister ruins perched upon a jagged mountain peak, the entire sight emphasised by sheer granite cliffs dropping precipitously no less than a thousand feet on three sides, as the Arges river curls below in wisps of mist rising almost continually.

The road to Castle Dracula winds through the green and brown foothills past stone huts painted pink, pale green, or yellow, around churches with curved steeples, shepherds in sheepskin cloaks and peaked caps and grandmothers in headkerchiefs and black skirts over stiff white petticoats. The road passes through Curtea de Arges, site of an ancient cathedral, and occasionally one sees shepherd boys on their carts and roving bands of gypsies. The climb begins from the village Capatineni where one encounters the horrified looks and also blessings of the superstitious local people.

The stern commanding air of the great pile, the majesty of its strategic, desolate location, and the wild beauty of its landscape are a sure invitation to any poet or artist. There could not possibly be a more apt setting for fearful crimes or mysterious hauntings. The upper portion of the trail is covered with wild flowers, luxuriant greenery and fungi; three quarters of the way down the valley, the black sweep of forest greets the eye. To its south the ruins command a panoramic vista of the Wallachian plain; to the north stand the snow-covered peaks of Fagaras mountains. Isolated thus on a remote precipice, Castle Dracula must have been virtually impregnable.

The spirit of Dracula seems to be best preserved in those sunken stones, Alpine weeds, snake holes and trails of masonry pebbles falling down to the river Arges. No other sound of life disturbs the quiet except the melancholy hooting of the owl, or the footfalls of a strayed and daring traveller. Within those ramparts, rats and mice abound, while the Romanian mountain bear is an occasional trespasser, as is the mountain lynx. The most dangerous visitor is the wolf; wild dogs often howl at night during the full moon - sending a shiver down the spine. The singular geography and bizarre design of the castle ruins make the wayfarer aware of its bloody past. Perhaps no other castle is filled with such awful memories. They say that evil spirits still haunt those ruins and the peasants of the valley speak of strange flickers, as of candle-light, being visible from a distance on dark nights.

I stared in a trance-like fashion in a cold, eerie mood;

remembered the vampire count and felt as if he had been waiting for us. A curious unease pervaded my soul as I gazed at the relic. I was overcome by a mysterious wistfulness, a sense of dreadful emptiness. This mood of foreboding was created by an intolerable gloom which engulfed my spirit. Time seemed to have stood still; a dense and impenetrable silence fell with an oppressive hush. There was something unutterably overpowering and disquieting about the place so weird and awesome. A dreadful fear overwhelmed me. I remembered Stoker: 'Supernatural, as if it had been transported from another world and planted stone by stone on this towering peak.' And the sense of the uncanny reminded me of Coleridge's:

> *A savage place, holy and enchanted*
>
> *That ever beneath a waning moon was haunted,*
>
> *By woman wailing for a demon lover.*

A few birds, not many, glided by the front wall, otherwise there was no sign of life, and nothing stirred. I looked around me: no cottages, no glimmer of lights, no blue smoke rising from chimneys, no sounds; the very stillness was frightening. To the south one beheld only the deep, twisting gorges of the Arges valley.

We felt as if we were being watched all the time. No one else was there of course, but we could sense an unearthly presence of evil. You could feel there was someone just around the corner. We were very, very scared. Truely, the shades of evil pervade this place even today, like an icy breath from the past. Stoker had already captured the atmosphere: The shadows are many and the wind breathes cold through the broken battlements, from whose tall windows came no ray of light.'

Architecturally the castle once combined the best characteristics of Teutonic and Byzantine fortifications. The walls, a patchwork of brick, stone and concrete, were an astounding six feet thick. The foundation was barely distinguishable from the granite rock on which it perched. Three ruined towers on the north wall and two deep dungeons seem to speak of a grim turbulent past and vanished glories. Those untidy heaps of stones, the crumbling towers where now only the nocturnal birds find refuge, were once doubly reinforced to resist the Turkish cannons, a proud and steadfast symbol of resistance to the outside invader.

As I stood there I could well imagine Jonathan Harker's attempt to escape from this dreadful prison, from this haunted fortress where he experienced many strange things, its atmosphere of magic, terror and horror, which drove him well to the verge of insanity. I recalled in Stoker's novel, Harker's peering out of his bedchamber window to ascertain whether some tremendous form might be ascending the sheer wall as the vampire count did. Or was that a trick of moonlight, or some weird effect of shadow? I saw the fingers and toes grasp the corners of the stones, just as a lizard moves along a wall.' Harker saw Dracula's head coming out of the window and he began to crawl down the castle wall over that dreadful abyss, *face down*, with his cloak spreading out around him like great wings. I stood rapt and amazed in the chamber where Harker may well have stayed and I too saw through the roofless window, the leaning wall, which still stands to this day with all its jutting stones.

The sight of the ruined turret reminded me of the tragic folk-tale concerning Dracula's wife who rushed up the winding staircase and hurled herself from the minaret into the river below: how her body must have rolled down the precipice into the flowing Arges! Professor McNally had told me that to this day that point of the river is called *Riul Doamei* or 'The Princess' River', a spot where the waters are reddened by a vague subterranean object, and the peasants say they have often heard the plaintive wailings of Dracula's wife rise from the gurgling waves.

Deep into the darkness peering

Long I stood there, wondering, fearing

Doubting, dreaming dreams,

No mortals ever dared to dream before.

Dracula's figure rises like a grim spectre from the past: how he sacked cities, decimated villages into ashes, and impaled thousands of Turks, Saxons, Germans and disloyal Romanians. 'The memory of bad princes,' writes Voltaire, 'is preserved like that of fires, plagues and inundations.' Dracula's contemporaries dreaded him as the living embodiment of Satan come as a scourge upon the earth; or like Faustus who sold his soul to the Devil in return for unlimited power, for surely he knew the secrets of life and death. He had known astrologers, alchemists and necromancers, and pursued his thirst for the unbounded occult.

Dracula is not the mythical product of a Victorian Irishman's lurid imagination. There was a factual basis for those fantasies. The legend of the vampire count and his mysterious nocturnal life relate to documented history, for Dracula did exist. He has been identified as Vlad Tepes the Impaler, who during the fifteenth century, after his mysterious escape from Turkish captors ascended the throne as Prince of Wallachia. A full account of his life, acts of cruelty and reign of terror, are contained in McNally and Florescu's fascinating study *In Search of Dracula*. Both authors have probed the folklore concerning this fearsome real-life prince and vampire, and established the true identity of this mysterious man and legend by researching into cracked and chipped fifteenth-century records, blurred manuscripts locked in the dust-laden vaults of ancient European monasteries, crudely lettered pamphlets mouldering in antique archives, and by charting the folk tales whispered in Slavic countries.

Philologists agreed at the sixth congress of onomastic sciences in Munich in 1958 that Stoker's *Dracula* can easily be identified with the historical personality of Vlad the Fifth of Wallachia, called the Impaler for his cruelties. He ruled from 1456 to 1462 and was briefly restored to his throne in 1476. Stoker only embroidered upon the historical Vlad Tepes and associated it with the local superstitions; his descriptions of the country and the castle, and of the river curling below the granite mountains, are amazingly accurate. And that's strange, because Stoker never visited Transylvania.

But before I investigate the sources and genesis of Stoker's *Dracula*, it would be apt to tell of an incident at the end of my expedition. The sun was low over the mountain-filled horizon, and there was not a breath of air when I began to retrace my steps down the valley to the highway below. Did I fancy that I heard something? I listened and there was the distinct sound of footfalls following me, but there was no one to be seen! Other members of my party had preceded me an hour before, while I had lingered on in the ruins to complete my notes. I have never been able to explain the echo of those footfalls, or the unseen, everwatchful presence, and I hurried on my way.

Like one, that on a lonesome road

Doth walk in fear and dread,

And having once turned round walks on

And turns no more his head

Because he knows, a frightful fiend

Doth close behind him tread.

The dark, blood-curdling vampire superstition is not a quaint folklore of Eastern Europe alone. The vampire is of dateless antiquity. In the dim corridors of time there is no more sinister figure than the living dead which prowls from its grave at night to drink the blood of the innocent and the beautiful. I have furnished a detailed history of the vampire-myth elsewhere. Although this myth has been much embellished in its poetic manifestations by literary artists, the vampire remains an embodiment of the Faustian quest to conquer eternity, a symbol and an image which transcend time and space.

The vampire stories have a hideous ring of realism. Hundreds of young maidens were found dead and drained of their lifeblood in the Carpathian valleys and lowlands of Hungary as the seventeenth century dawned. Public records reveal that in 1732, in Serbia and Wallachia, vampirism spread like pestilence causing numerous deaths. There had been a notorious case of vampirism near Belgrade in 1731. As the century drew to its close, reports of dead returning from the grave multiplied alarmingly.

Such incidents coincided with church-inspired bulletins that Vampires were excommunicated persons whom the Earth is said to cast up.' The church also documented complex rituals for protection against vampires: the weapons of attack were garlic, the Cross and Communion Wafers. Excommunication from the church was an infallible method of turning into a vampire. A case of suicide inevitably guaranteed 'the sleep of the undead'. Those who were denied full and proper burial rights, or passed away apostate or unbaptised, or persons who had feasted upon the meat of a sheep killed by a wolf, or even those who had lived an immoral, evil life, were supposed to turn into vampires.

Dracula lived at a time when there was a widespread belief in vampires. Outbreaks of plague and premature burials were quite prevalent. It was not uncommon to see a body rise from a cart while being driven to the cemetery. Catalepsy often resulted in premature burial and 'corpses' would stir and revive in a shallow grave. The peasants practised the ritual of exhuming the dead. Twisted bodies in crypts and coffins would provide proof that the body had been possessed by a vampire. Even to this day, in Transylvania, stakes are driven through the hearts of the dead to keep them in their graves.

Vampire bats are a common phenomenon in the Carpathians, and their victims exhibit symptoms of rabies. People with bat wounds become demented and wish to bite others, and usually die within weeks. Such symptoms of hydrophobia concord well with the Dracula vampire myth. On the authority of Montague Summers, cases of vampirism seem to happen every day, but they are hushed up. As recent as 1970, there have been reported cases from England, Sumatra and elsewhere.

There has not yet been any valid or thoroughgoing research upon the sources of Stoker and the genesis of *Dracula*. He had, of course, seen the torture tower of the old castle at Nuremberg. His brother George, once a surgeon in London, had in Turkey, gained experience in handling human corpses. Irving, whom Stoker served, himself had been vampire-like, draining those who worked with him. But Stoker's fascination with vampirism, already stimulated by Sheridan Le Fanu's *Carmilla,*was rekindled in the 1890s by his meeting in the Beefsteak Room, with a professor from the Hungarian University of Budapest who had the exotic name Arminius Vambery. It has been surmised that he elaborated to Stoker some details of Transylvanian superstitions and mentioned the strange Wallachian Prince 'Viovode Drakula' who had ruled in 1456 and was called 'The Impaler' because of his ravenous activities. Vambery showed Stoker a fifteenth-century manuscript which referred to him as a 'Wampyr'.

Daniel Farson, a prolific writer and broadcaster, and a grandnephew of Bram Stoker, has stated that the opening chapters of *Dracula* were written at Cruden Bay, a small fishing village north of Aberdeen, where Stoker stayed during a walking tour in 1893, and then returned each year during the off seasons from the Lyceum Theatre to relax. Cruden Bay is much the same today and has not been caught up in modern progress; there are still small fishermen's cottages dotting the seashore and fishing-nets stretched on high poles like a series of black tents. And there is even a ruined castle lashed by the sea! To the north of Cruden Bay rise great rocks of red granite, jagged and broken, and the stormy sea often blasts upon the rocks in grand fury. We can fancy Stoker striding across the sands of Cruden, and as Harry Ludlam notes: 'To the sound of the sea on the Scottish shore, Count Dracula made his entry.' But there were other influences.

The carved vampire fangs and canine teeth of Tibetan and Nepalese images of gods shed strange light on the origin of vampire legends. Did the tales of weird beings who subsisted by drinking the blood of sleeping persons originate in Transylvania, or with the Hindus of ancient India? Clues concerning the Indian origin were provided by a prominent orientalist. Sir Richard Burton, the nineteenth-century translator of the *Arabian Nights*. In 1870, Sir Richard had translated eleven vampire tales of apparent Indian origin from a thoroughly Hindu legend composed in Sanskrit, the ancient and sacred language of India. Sir Richard thought that these tales inspired future writing of 'facetious, fictitious literature'.

Tibetan manuscripts concerning vampires were 'held in such high regard that they were embalmed in images to increase their sanctity.' My findings on these researches are contained in my Introduction on 'The Vampire in Legend, Lore, and Literature', prefixed to the 1970 Arno edition of T P Brest's *Varney the Vampire; or The Feast of Blood*.

On 13th August 1878, Sir Henry Irving arrived by train at the Westland Row Station, Dublin, accompanied by Richard Burton. It was on that railway platform that

Irving introduced Stoker to Burton who had been to Mecca. Stoker writes:

> The man riveted my attention. He was dark and forceful, and masterful and ruthless. I have never seen so iron a countenance... He is steel! He would go through you like a sword!

In January 1879, Stoker saw Burton again in London with Irving in the Green Room Club. The first supper at Irving's rooms in Grafton Street on Saturday night, 8th February has thus been recorded by Stoker:

> The subdued light and the quietude gave me a better opportunity of studying Burton's face;... I sat opposite to him and not beside him. The predominant characteristics were the darkness of the face - desert burning; the strong mouth and nose, and jaw and forehead - the latter somewhat bold - and the strong, deep, resonant voice. My first impression of the man as of steel was consolidated and enhanced.

That night Burton talked about many things including the translation of the *Arabian Nights*, a task of extensive magnitude and demanding research.

During the next meeting on Saturday, 15th February, the evening chat veered round Burton's experiences on the west coast of Africa, 'The Gold Coast,' where he was consul and where he sustained his good health by *never going out in the mid-day sun* and by drinking *a whole flask of brandy every day!* But the third supper on 21st February, at Bailey's Hotel, South Kensington, arranged by Mr Mullen the publisher, was most interesting, especially when Burton mentioned experiences, or expounded grounds for some theory which he held.

Burton narrated 'some of his explorations amongst old tombs'.

While posted as consul in Damascus, Burton had developed a new passion for archaeology, and he seemed to lavish upon the ancient dead all the inquisitiveness he had devoted to the living in India and Africa. He had spent weeks in the Syrian mountains, searching for skulls, bones and inscriptions while mapping ruins. Stoker writes:

> Burton's face seemed to lengthen when he laughed; the upper lip rising instinctively and showing the right canine tooth. This was always a characteristic of his enjoyment.

After a lapse of nearly six years Stoker met Burton again. On 9th July 1886, Irving invited Sir Richard and Lady Burton to supper in the Beefsteak Room after the staging of *Faust*. Burton described his clandestine and dangerous visit to Mecca in the disguise of an Arab. A lad recognised him and quietly slipped away to pass on information, but Burton took the situation in hand and having pursued the lad to a solitary corner suddenly drove a polard into his heart! When Burton described this incident at dinner, there fell a hush and muffled silence; then some guests got up from the table and walked out of the room. Burton continued in his resonant voice:

> The desert has its own laws, and there - supremely of all the East - to kill is a small offence. In any case what could I do? It had to be his life or mine!

Stoker notes that as Burton spoke 'the upper lip rose and his canine tooth showed its full length like the gleam of a dagger.' Indeed Burton had a most vivid way of narrating incidents, especially of the East. He was gifted with a fine imaginative power and a memory richly stored by study and bizarre experiences. Stoker asserts that:

> Burton *knew* the East. Its brilliant dawns and sunset; its rich tropic vegetation, and its fiery arid deserts; its cool, dark mosques and temples; its crowded bazaars; its narrow streets; its windows guarded for outlooking and from in-looking eyes; the pride and swagger of its passionate men, and the mysteries of its veiled women; its romances; its beauty; its horrors.

And it was on 18th September 1886, as night wore on, that Burton's fancy seemed to run riot in all its alluring power, and the whole world of thought seemed to flame with gorgeous colour. He talked of unknown places of the earth and of some unspeakable mysterious secrets. This excellent swordsman and archaeologist who had revelled in *Arabian Nights* and translated several volumes of the oriental erotica, had surely heard the story of the strange Prince of Wallachia and the Carpathian legends from the descendants of those merchants and carpet-sellers of Damascus who had supplied rugs and furs and decorative motifs to Vlad Dracula for his castle.

It was Burton who further passed on those whispered folk-tales and legends to Bram Stoker. And the image of Dracula caught the fancy of Stoker - the image of a handsome, bloodthirsty outlandish prince in his embroidered shirt, ermine cape, and a headgear plumed with ostrich feathers!

Professor Oswald Doughty writing his book on Gabriel Rossetti makes the point that 'Exhumation of the passionately loved dead had become quite a literary fashion,' and quotes instances from Victorian life and society. In 1862, Rossetti's wife Lizzie committed suicide by taking an overdose of laudanum. On the second and third days following her death, so lifelike was her appearance - perhaps because of some preservative ingredient of the drug - that Gabriel refused to believe her dead and insisted upon a last opinion of the coroner before she could be buried in Highgate Cemetery.

There is a touching story that tells of Rossetti placing a little red-edged manuscript book of verses, bound in rough grey calf, poems that were inspired and addressed to his wife, in the coffin near the face of the dead beloved, wrapped round in the flowing tresses of her beautiful golden hair. Seven and a half years after her burial, he exhumed her body to recover the manuscript which he had sealed in her grave.

That early October evening of 1869 in Highgate Cemetery must have been a scene at once macabre and strange: Lizzie's open coffin reflected in the light of a great fire made beside the grave as protection against infection. Lizzie's body, it is reported, was still wonderfully preserved, perhaps still the effect of the drug which had proved fatal. Hall Caine writes: 'the body was apparently quite perfect on coming to the light of the fire on the surface, and when the book was lifted, there came away some of the beautiful golden hair in which Rossetti had entwined it.' The manuscript glowing in the red light of the fire, emerged from the sealed doors of the tomb.

Those who were present must have gazed with an intense elation upon the form of an almost legendary figure, and wondered at the famed golden hair which was to become a source of so much Pre-Raphaelite inspiration. News gradually leaked out that Lizzie's hair had continued to grow after her death, long, beautiful and most luxuriant, so as to fill the coffin with its burning gold! And was Stoker, a friend of Hall Caine, unaware of all this happening during his life and times?

Christopher Lee as Count Dracula

A VAMPIRE TALISMAN

My friend Montague Summers gave me lots of advice in case I should ever meet a ghost or vampire and in particular he gave me a seventeenth-century East European medallion or talisman that he assured me had laid to rest scores of vampires. It has been suggested that this pious and learned Roman Catholic believed completely in vampires *because* he wanted to believe in them - that the thought that such things really existed made life more exciting; but there is surely more to it than that.

The Reverend Alphonsus Joseph-Mary Augustus Montague Summers MA, FRSL, was born in 1880 and educated at Clifton College and Trinity College, Oxford. He spent much of his life abroad, notably in Italy, but in London he founded a society devoted to producing old plays. He superintended the production of eighteen himself as well as a complete Congreve season and other revivals.

He was the author of over thirty books and several plays; he edited a score more and translated and edited yet more, including *Malleus Maleficarum* (The Hammer of Witches') in 1926 and *A Treatise of Ghosts* in 1933. His own books included *An Appreciation of Jane Austen*, bibliographies of Restoration Drama and the Gothic Novel, but he is best known for his monumental works on *The Werewolf* (1933), *The Vampire: His Kith and Kin* (1928) and *The Vampire in Europe* (1929).

After his retirement from the priesthood he became an acknowledged expert throughout the world on black magic and kindred subjects; a firm believer in the supernatural, in miracles and in ghosts. He was a man who listed among his recreations 'the investigation of occult phenomena,' 'talking to intelligent dogs, that is, all dogs,' and 'ghost stories.'

We had exchanged several letters and eventually I went to see him at his home on Richmond Green. I am not sure what I expected but I found a tall and stately man with flowing silver hair; a kindly man who did much to awaken my interest in the occult.

At the time I had come across a case of apparent vampirism and I found Summers tremendously helpful with knowledgeable advice. But all my efforts to countermand my vampire had no effect and some weeks after my initial visit I was back talking to him again. This time he brought out a brass medallion which he said had great power against vampires and evil spirits. He said that he did not expect to have any further use for it but he wanted it to be in the possession of someone who could use it whenever the necessity arose.

He believed completely in the supernatural vampire and had no doubt whatever that I would be called upon to use the talisman many times during my lifetime. He blessed it for me and told me that its effectiveness would deteriorate if its power was publicised. He died suddenly soon afterwards and I have never had occasion to use the medallion in the quarter-century or more since it has been in my possession.

I feel that it is unlikely that I shall now be asked to call upon the powers associated with this strange medallion - the history of which I know very little - and I feel that I owe it to Montague Summers and perhaps to the sceptics of vampirism to relate some of the reputed successes of this object; but first let me describe it.

The heavy brass talisman measures eight centimetres from top to bottom, five-and-three-quarter centimetres at its widest part and weighs two ounces. It appears to be made of brass or brass alloy and consists of a circular medal surmounted by two eagle-like birds chained by the neck, each looking in opposite directions.

Both sides of the medal contain lettering in what

could be old Slavonic, or Romanian, which incorporated both Roman and Cyrillic characters; it has yet to be translated. In the centre of the medal the obverse side bears the head of a man who has the distinctive nose, the staring eyes and the long face that is revealed on all the reputed portraits of Dracula. The figure appears to be clothed and the head protected by some kind of chain mail and the head seems to be crowned with a row of seven precious stones. Around the neck there is a similar row of seven circular stones. On the left-hand side of the head is a circle over a cross and on the right-hand side a design that could be a brand of fire.

The reverse of the medallion depicts a curious man-like figure with a birdlike head and wearing a conical cap and some form of mail encasing the whole body. In one hand the figure grasps the blade of a sword and in the other a pointed stake; both point downwards.

There is an eighteenth-century Hungarian vampire case that is recounted by Summers in his book *The Vampire: His Kith and Kin*. He told me the medallion had been used on that occasion but this is the first time that the part played by the medallion has been published.

The vampire had been terrorising the Hungarian village for several years and although its lair had been traced to the local churchyard, no one had felt capable of attempting to placate the vampire - or in Magyar, the *Vampir*.

A vampire-hunter heard of the trouble and armed with the medallion arrived at the village. Having ascertained from the local people that a vampire was in fact active and that it had its lair in the cemetery, he offered to rid the village of the pest. In order to see the whole churchyard he climbed the clock tower of the church and from that vantage point watched for the appearance of the vampire. When he saw the vampire emerge from its tomb, he noticed that it shed its coffin shroud and grave clothes before making its way to the village.

When the vampire was out of sight the vampire-hunter, the protective talisman around his neck, descended the tower, made his way to the vampire's grave, gathered up the grave clothes in his arms and hastened back to the comparative safety of the church tower.

On returning to its grave and finding the shroud and linen missing, the vampire searched in vain among the gravestones and then spotted the culprit at the top of the church tower.

Waving the clothes, the vampire-hunter indicated that the vampire must come and fetch them if he wished to recover the clothing and the vampire, it is recorded, began to climb the steep and dangerous stairway that led to the tower. Evidently he wished the vampire-hunter to believe that he was a normal being and therefore did not resort to supernatural means of ascending the tower, such as climbing up the wall or changing into a bat.

At the last bend before the top the vampire-hunter was ready for him and suddenly he darted out and confronted the vampire with the medallion held at arm's length in the face of the vampire. As though he had been struck a heavy blow the vampire fell over and over down the stone stairway. The vampire-hunter followed and was able to decapitate the vampire before it had recovered from its fall and so put an end to that particular vampire.

In 1909 (twelve years after *Dracula* was published) a vampire apparently terrorised a district in Dracula country - Southern Transylvania - and following a sharp increase in sudden deaths in the area with bodies being drained of blood, Montague Summers, in Italy at the time, heard about the case and hurried to see what he could do. He told me that after great difficulty he gained admittance to a castle occupied by a powerful landowner. Professing a deep interest in the history and architecture of the castle Summers talked with the owner, a cold and silent individual who never moved from his chair all the time Summers was with him.

Eventually Summers steered the conversation to legend and folklore and to belief in vampirism, then the talk of the whole district. Summer's host pooh-poohed the idea of a vampire causing the mysterious deaths but when Summers, casually during the course of conversation, brought out the vampire protection medal, the effect was instantaneous. The man's eyes blazed for a moment with anger - or fright - he shrank back and then, recovering himself he fixed his hypnotic eyes on Summers who immediately felt his strength ebbing away but he summoned all his strength and picking up the medal, he held it at arm's length before his face for protection.

The man he was confronting covered his eyes, turned away and rang for his servant who summarily showed Summers out of the castle. Believing that he had proved his power to the vampire Summers prepared to comfort the villagers and tell them that they would not be troubled further since he reasoned that the vampire would not risk further confrontation with him and the medal, but he was too late.

That night the villagers surrounded the castle and set it on fire; the castle and all its occupants perished. As Montague Summers put it to me: 'No vampire could possibly withstand the sight of this medal and fire on the same night!'

There are many other accounts of the use of this ancient amulet and I have an open mind on its power but that it is very old and very strange there can be no doubt. If any of my readers are troubled by vampires I will be pleased to test its powers in these days of unbelief...

The black Dracula *Blacula* (1973)

VAMPIRES AND HIGHGATE CEMETERY

The oldest part of Highgate Cemetery has long been reputed to harbour a vampire and what a place for a vampire to 'rest'; with its forty-five thousand graves, forgotten and forsaken tombs, overgrown paths and atmosphere of utter and complete ruin and decay wherever you walk.

Alleged sightings of a vampire-like creature - a grey spectre - lurking among the graves and tombstones have resulted in many 'Vampire hunts'; some of which landed those taking part in the hands of the police.

In 1968, I heard first-hand of such a sighting and my informant maintained that he and his companion had secreted themselves in one of the vaults and watched a dark figure flit among the catacombs and disappear into a huge vault from which the vampire, ghost or whatever it may have been, did not reappear. Subsequent search revealed no trace inside the vault but I was told that a trail of drops of blood stopped at an area of massive coffins which could have hidden a dozen vampires.

Other reports in 1968 and 1969 told of a similar figure visiting various graves and appearing and disappearing in circumstances that ruled out the possibility of the figure being human. One man told me that he had seen 'something' emerge from a coffin inside a vault and then disappear and a moment later his companions, outside the vault, had seen a figure materialise seemingly from the ground and disappear with incredible speed and swift, long strides, along one of the lonely pathways in the cemetery.

A number of passers-by have seen figures flitting hither and thither among the tombs and a motorist whose car broke down near one of the cemetery gates reported seeing 'something' peer at him through the iron gates and then speed away into the dim reaches of the cemetery so fast that he could not believe that it had been anything human. His recollection of the 'thing' that looked at him was of staring eyes and white teeth disclosed by what he described as a snarl.

Correspondents in my own postbag and in newspapers have maintained that a vampire, probably a Wallachian nobleman in the Middle Ages, had been brought to England in a coffin of his native earth by his followers at the beginning of the eighteenth century. It was suggested that he had been placed in Highgate Cemetery and that the place had been the centre of vampirism in Europe ever since.

Publicity of a dubious kind has surrounded the activities of a person or persons named Farrant and his - or their - association with Highgate Cemetery, in search of vampires.

In 1970 a Mr *David* Farrant of Archway Road, Highgate, said, during the course of a television interview, that he planned to seek out the vampire in the cemetery and put an end to it be driving a stake through its heart.

A history teacher from Chelmsford (with the appropriate name of Blood) is described in a contemporary newspaper report as an 'expert on vampirism' and he met Farrant and they exchanged ideas. Blood became convinced that Farrant's ideas would attract too much publicity and too many people for any self-respecting vampire to put in an appearance and, convinced beyond doubt that a vampire of evil appearance did in fact haunt the cemetery. Blood said he would search for the creature by himself at dawn.

Meanwhile David Farrant's broadcast had attracted a good deal of attention and scores of people excitedly climbed one of the high walls surrounding the cemetery and proceeded, somewhat noisily, to seek out the vampire. Not a few of them returned to their companions in the roadway rather shaken and maintaining that they had seen 'something' in the dark patches between some of the tombs. The overpopulated hunt fizzled out inconclusively.

A few days later Mr Blood tried his hand at finding the elusive vampire of Highgate Cemetery and he had no more success than David Farrant who seemingly carried out yet another attempt at running the creature to earth. However it transpired that amateurs were shooting a film in the cemetery about this time - and the origin of certain rumours and stories of 'unexplained' figures and shapes may well have been in the activities of the actors and those involved in filming *Vampires at Night;* although David Farrant remained convinced that he had encountered an inexplicable form, dark and ominous, in the shape of a human being, that glided rather than walked over the corpse-laden ground of the cemetery where, he thought, vaults had been damaged during his sojourn. He saw the strange shape no less than four times and told newspaper reporters that he was convinced that there was something evil in the cemetery that manifested itself on occasions.

Six months later a Mr *Allan* Farrant was caught climbing over the wall of Highgate Cemetery carrying a wooden cross and a sharpened stake of wood. He was described as a hospital orderly with an address in Manor Road, Barnet. He was, apparently, intent on vampire-hunting and felt certain that he would meet a vampire that night for the moon was full and he seemed in no doubt that a bloodsucking vampire walked the cemetery at night and lay in its coffin by day.

'I won't rest until I catch the vampire,' he told police and he had every intention of stalking the vampire once he sighted it, and following it back to its lair in a catacomb. In reporting this incident the Baltimore *Sun* of 30th September 1970, commented that apparently it was not illegal to hunt vampires in Britain.

'Then,' Allan Farrant told the court, 'I would have gone into the catacomb, searched through the coffins until I recognised the vampire and then I would have driven my wooden stake through his heart.'

The Clerkenwell magistrate, Mr D Prys-Jones, before whom Allan Farrant appeared charged with entering enclosed premises for an unlawful purpose, dismissed the case after Mr Jeffrey Bays, who appeared for Allan Farrant, pointed out that there was no evidence put forward to say that his client's beliefs were not true beliefs. 'People have spent fortunes looking for the Loch Ness Monster and other serpents,' Mr Bays continued, 'and there is no less truth in her existence than in my client's beliefs.'

According to the *Daily Mail* Allan Farrant saw 'an apparition' eight feet tall in the cemetery that 'just floated along the ground' when he was on watch one morning waiting 'for the vampire to rise'. He believed that there had been a vampire in Highgate Cemetery for about ten years and he said he had founded an organisation a few years earlier with a hundred members throughout Britain and in Europe who were searching for vampires.

Less than a month later a Mr *David* Farrant was guiding Barry Simmons of the London *Evening News* on a night-tour of Highgate Cemetery armed with cross and wooden stake which he carried under his arm in a paper carrier bag. In fact the whole project seems to have been a somewhat dismal and depressing effort - even the cross, created from two pieces of wood, was tied together with a shoelace.

However what may have been missing in organisation and perfection in equipment seems to have been made up for in enthusiasm and, according to reports, David Farrant and Barry Simmons stalked: cross in one hand to ward off the evil spirits and stake in the other, held at the ready to strike terror into even a vampire. They stalked among the vaults and graves, among the dark bushes and beside the shadowy walls and when they had completed the tour, they began again. They found no vampire.

What they did find was evidence of the tremendous damage that has been done to the cemetery in recent years. Dozens of graves have been disturbed and bodies moved; sometimes skulls and other remains have been stolen. Vaults have been defaced with strange scrawls and coffins broken into. Even the lead of some coffins has been plundered and the total damage has been estimated at well over ten thousand pounds.

For a time David Farrant kept watch at Highgate Cemetery every night and although he heard stories of graves being desecrated and in particular of one account of some schoolgirls finding the body of a woman that had been dragged from a tomb - with a stake through her heart - he did not see the vampire or any other 'apparition'. If he did not trace the vampire to its lair he was not discouraged. 'He is evil and has to be destroyed,' David Farrant was reported to have said at the time. 'There is no question of giving up. We have got to carry on until this thing is destroyed.'

In February 1974 a Mr *Robert* Farrant of Archway Road, Highgate, was charged with unlawfully possessing a .38 revolver and ammunition and stealing pillow cases, a sheet, blankets and a towel from Barnet General Hospital. He was further charged with removing a body from Highgate Cemetery; the body of a man having been found in a car near the cemetery. In July 1974 David Robert Farrant was found guilty of damaging a memorial at Highgate cemetery, breaking open catacombs there and interfering with the remains of bodies. He was sentenced to four years eight months imprisonment.

Ever since I became aware that Highgate Cemetery was the reputed haunt of a vampire, the investigations and activities of Mr Sean Manchester commanded my attention. I became convinced that, more than anyone else, this psychic consultant and President of The British Occult Society, knew the full story of the Highgate Vampire and I am delighted to be able to include his remarkable contribution as a separate chapter in this book for it provides a startling account of present-day vampirism by a researcher into the field of occultism who, like all true researchers, looks first for a rational explanation. Sometimes, however, no such explanation is forthcoming.

THE HIGHGATE VAMPIRE

by Sean Manchester

As it has been my destiny to explore those aspects of the occult which by their very nature defy all attempts at logical explanation and scientific examination, and having had the unique though sometimes harrowing experience of discovering a facet of the malign supernatural thought to have vanished centuries ago if it existed at all, the task now befalls me, at the request of Peter Underwood, to commit pen to paper and attempt a brief description of those incredible events of late.

Circumstances have brought me to many a strange, unchartered place in my endeavours as an occult investigator, but the case I am about to relate found those involved standing on the threshold of a vast, shadowy world - the existence of which the materialistic mind denies altogether and the surface of which has barely been scratched at all by researchers. It is a case which deals with one of those borderland subjects which had not been sufficiently examined and studied before it was dumped on the quagmire of exploded superstitions by modern researchers. A subject which, nevertheless, holds a fearful fascination and instils uneasiness in its most ardent critic.

Since the beginning of time men have hoped and believed in life after death. Attempts to contact the dead have been frequent and varied. The question still haunts us - is there a world beyond death? A world of spirits, demons and the dead who do not rest quietly in their bony dust... vampires!

Having always had a passion for strange and mysterious places that lie one step beyond the world we all know, my interest was more than aroused on hearing of the Highgate phenomenon which was at the time being taken for a ghost: it was like finding an undiscovered country waiting to be explored. Who would have thought then that I was on the trail of the Highgate Vampire!

At the beginning of my investigation I was extremely reluctant to even mention the word 'Vampire', but as enquiries proceeded it became increasingly difficult to avoid; indeed, as the evidence amassed its omission was noticeable by its absence; as if it had been staring me in the face all the time. But, during those early weeks and months, it was imperative that I retain an objective, critical mind. After all, this was twentieth-century London, not a remote area of south-east Europe in the dark ages. However, as the evidence became unearthed, all the years of disbelief of things which lie beyond the confines of science were, for those who encountered it, suddenly washed away.

Before proceeding further with this account I feel it necessary to make abundantly clear to the reader what a vampire is by my definition. I do this because the word Vampire' in recent years has gained a broader meaning which is extended to include blood-lusting psychotics who, though possessing vampiric qualities, remain very much part of the living. Also, 'psychic vampires' who drain their victims of energy through the power of the mind have been included under the heading.

The German witch, Clara Geisslerin, was tried in 1597 for exhuming dead children in order to drink their blood. Countess Elizabeth Bathory (as we have seen) died in the darkness of Csejthe Castle, Hungary, in 1614 after drinking and bathing in the blood of six hundred and fifty girls over a period of several years. More recently, in 1886, Henri Blot was accused in Paris of performing necrophilia (sexual intercourse with a corpse) on the newly-dead bodies of two young women and was jailed for two years. Fritz Haarmann, however, was executed in 1925 for committing twenty-seven vampiric murders; as was Peter Kur-ten in 1931 for strangling, raping and cutting the throats of twenty-nine victims. More recently still, John Haigh, the so-called 'Vampire of London', confessed to killing his victims, then making an incision in the side of the neck whereupon he would collect the blood in a glass and drink it or even drink directly from the wound.

Despite the vampiric qualities of these sadistic and psychotic people who suffered largely from haematodipsia (a sexual thirst for blood), they are nowhere as fearful as their supernatural counterpart. The true vampire is a dead body re-animated during the blackest hours of night to prey upon the blood of the living. Sharing the dark and terrible qualities of both ghost and demon, the vampire cannot die, but must go on adding new victims to satiate its need for blood.

The *Oxford Dictionary* describes a vampire as 'a ghost that leaves his grave at night and sucks the blood of sleeping persons.' This is what I am talking about when I use the word 'Vampire': a supernatural being, belonging neither to the living nor the dead, who emerges from the nightmare world of the undead to quaff fresh blood whereby it is nourished and revitalised. We shall try and grasp an understanding of the 'undead' condition presently, but first let the reader be in no doubt as to how very well-documented vampirism was before it had been consigned to the rubbish-heap of exploded myths by twentieth-century science.

In fact the ravages of the vampire in the Middle Ages left no European country untouched. Records tell of graves being discovered saturated with squelching blood during vampire epidemics. Needless to say, local folk and in particular the clergy were kept busy employing the ancient and approved methods necessary to rid themselves of this abhorrent evil.

Earlier still, indications of the existence of the vampire are to be found throughout Greek, Roman and Jewish history. The Babylonians knew and feared the vampire, as did people throughout Asia, Africa and Europe. The more materialistic minds of today have shut the door on the subject and what might have been cases of vampirism ceased to be recorded as such many years ago.

Though many attempts have been made and will continue to be made to explain away the undead phenomenon, by far the favourite piece of rationalisation on the part of the nonbelievers is the 'premature burial' theory. The theory suggests that in the case of exhumation where vampirism has been suspected, the discovery of a fresh and bloodstained body only indicates that it was buried alive.

A person suffering from catalepsy or in an advanced state of coma which exhibits all the signs and symptoms of death would, it is supposed, recover inside the coffin and frantically tear at the inside of the lid, cutting the hands in the process - hence the blood. This would also explain the fearful expression on the face of the exhumed corpse. A good, logical theory which slams the door on the possibility of a supernatural answer, until, that is, we examine it more closely. Then the door between us and another world slowly creaks open again.

Someone in a cataleptic trance or deep coma still needs some air and the amount trapped in a coffin when interred is very limited. That there might be enough air to allow such a person to regain consciousness and put up such a fierce struggle that they bleed badly is highly doubtful. In the case of premature burials, of which there has been a considerable number in past centuries, the eventual death of the unfortunate person would only be delayed by a matter of hours. Yet the vampire, when exhumed after months, years or even centuries, will show no trace of decomposition, but rather appear as if in a profound sleep.

It has also been suggested that an artificially preserved body if disinterred could easily be mistaken for a vampire. However, when a true vampire is exhumed it will be found to be remarkably fresh and of a clear complexion, betraying a trickle of blood at the corners of its mouth. Moreover, when the stake pierces the heart, fresh blood will jet and spurt forth in all directions as the quivering, writhing body shudders to a halt. An embalmed corpse cannot possibly betray bloodstains.

Another point that all scientific explanations overlook is that when a vampire is exorcised it will emit a blood-curdling scream and, where many years have elapsed, will turn immediately to dust due to true age.

To begin to understand the vampire at all, one must first relate in terms of the impossible become possible: a world where there is life in death. If the condition known as 'undead' is fully grasped, then we can begin to grow aware of the actuality of vampirism. If we think of vampires merely in terms of phenomena belonging only to past centuries, we deceive ourselves.

Vampires have the ability to remain undead indefinitely if not exorcised in a precise manner. We, on the other hand, age by the moment. As we pass to each moment, the previous moment has gone for ever. And, like any creature, we eventually die. With the undead, however, this is not the case. They live outside of time; therefore, when discovered after centuries, a vampire might only appear three score years in age.

We are familiar with only three dimensions and the sequence of before, now and after. This restricts us enormously when trying to comprehend the world of the undead. Our earthly bodies move in time. The vampire's does not, but is trapped in a twilight hell between life and death. From this there is only one escape by which the tormented soul may be released to find the peace of death. Only one way.

Vampire belief in itself presupposes a belief in the existence of God and, of course, the devil: the vampire being manifest through the power of evil. It must be realised that the link between this world and the undead world is found in Satanism, black magic and devil worship. Indeed, those devotees sufficiently wicked to merit the devil's partiality will probably continue their evil ambitions and selfish passions beyond the grave as the devil's emissaries. It is hardly surprising that such persons do not rest undisturbed in their graves after setting into action such malevolent forces.

The revival of the darker aspects of occultism in recent years, not least of all diabolism, has created ideal conditions for the propagation of vampirism. Down the ages Satanists have practised their evil craft and worshipped the devil in the hope of gaining powers, especially powers beyond the grave. They have always been with us, casting dark and ominous shadows throughout history, but their influence has never been stronger, since, perhaps, the Renaissance, than it is today. That black magic is attracting increasing interest and, regrettably, support, can no longer be held in doubt. A *Daily Mirror* inquiry into the subject on 28th February 1972 estimated that there are ten thousand black witches in Britain who worship evil.

The repeal of the ancient Witchcraft Act in 1951 allowed covens to gain recruits without hindrance. The last decade has witnessed a sharp increase in the number of occurrences directly attributed to devil worship.

The London *Evening Standard* on 1st November 1968 reported:

> *Graves disturbed, coffins dug up and prised open, crosses broken and the remains of a midnight Witch's Sabbat - that was the scene today at a London cemetery where devil worshippers held Hallowe'en rites last night. The superintendent, who is a clergyman, and is also chaplain, said, 'I've never seen anything like it. It isn't just ordinary vandalism. Everything has been carefully done, and arranged according to some evil rite. There's more in this than meets the eye. I believe some kind of Black Magic ceremony has been held here - and it's not the first time.'*

Bizarre desecrations and evidence of profane ceremonies have become almost commonplace in recent years and feelings that a witchcraft revival was in evidence were echoed in the London *Evening News*, 6th February 1969:

> *Fears of a dramatic revival in witchcraft in Kent and Sussex increased today with the discovery of three more acts of desecration in isolated cemeteries. In most of the cases gravestones had been smashed, stone crosses pulled to the ground and signs daubed in green paint on the graves.*

A local newspaper in north London, the *Islington Gazette*, had this to say in its editorial on 29th January 1971:

> *It seems strange that in these allegedly enlightened days that Black Magic should be said to be on the increase. We hear reports of strange happenings in graveyards and in local churches; reports of ceremonies that would have been better forgotten about and left with the rest of the superstition and barbarity of the Middle Ages.*

Why, indeed, should the practice of black magic with its emergent blood rituals and barbaric goings-on be growing so rapidly in our highly sophisticated society? It would be quite impossible to deal adequately with so vast a subject as the black arts with all its diverse ramifications here. Sufficient perhaps for the present that the reader understands that Satanism is a cause; the effect of which can sometimes be vampirism.

When my investigation of the Highgate Vampire began, I entertained no illusions as to the difficulties involved. Natural explanations were sought before considering supernatural ones in those early days, but each step more enshrined the proceedings in the latter. Each new discovery brought with it echoes of another world. Those uncanny events I now wish to record omitting lengthy analysis that would prove tedious for the average reader, but retaining, nevertheless, all relevant and essential information.

At my disposal are diaries, documents, photographs, tape-recordings, and the files and records of the British Occult Society, an organisation for psychical research and occult studies, of which I have the privilege to serve as President. My task would have been easier and more comprehensible to the reader if it was possible to disclose everything in its entirety, but there must be limitations where confidences are involved and I have to omit using names in full where requested.

The following account, then, deals with a subject, the serious discussion of which is not only avoided by the majority of people generally, but by the greater percentage of psychical researchers too.

Ignoring such phenomena, however, does nothing to ensure its departure.

***

Two seemingly unconnected incidents occurred within weeks of one another in the early months of 1967 that were to bring the Highgate phenomenon to my attention. Though at the time I paid no special attention to them, I could not help my interest being aroused by their strange nature. In the light of what was to follow they proved even more eerie. And alarming.

The first involved two sixteen-year-old pupils of La Sainte Union Convent, Highgate. They were walking home at night after having visited friends in Highgate Village. Their journey took them down Swains Lane past Highgate Cemetery. Barbara and Elizabeth, both intelligent schoolgirls, were not inclined to believe their eyes at first as they passed the north gate of the cemetery; for in front of them, amid the jungle of jutting tombstones and decaying mausoleums, dead bodies were emerging from their graves. The two girls continued walking in eerie silence until they reached the bottom of the lane where they spoke for the first time, having found their voices, and discovered they had both experienced the same weird scene.

The following account was given to me by Elizabeth Wojdyla, one of the schoolgirls, some months later:

Normally going past the cemetery, when you're just in a normal mood, you can feel the evil presence from the old cemetery. But this time my friend and I were coming down from Highgate Village and we were really in a great mood: we had just been to see a girlfriend and we were happy. We were not talking, just walking. And we were walking down, having just passed the north gate, when we both saw this scene of graves directly in front of us. And the graves were opening up; and the people were rising. We were not conscious of walking down the lane. We were only conscious of this graveyard scene.

For some time afterwards, Elizabeth was troubled by a series of nightmares all with one thing in common: something evil was trying to come in through her bedroom window at night. She could see the face clearly; it was deathly white. Just like the faces of the corpses leaving their graves. In the mornings, as the light of a new day poured through those panes that had previously framed an unknown horror in her dreams, Elizabeth felt silly at being frightened of such things. After all, no actual harm came to her and the nightmares eventually ceased.

Was this convent schoolgirl in possession of extrasensory perception, or was everything imagined? If an illusion, it is interesting to remember that her friend, Barbara, experienced an identical one. She did not, however, suffer the nightmares as described by Elizabeth.

A passage from *The Catholic Encyclopedia*, though not altogether consolatory, helped make the girls feel a little less silly: 'The Church does not deny that, with special permission of God, the souls of the departed may appear to the living, and even manifest things unknown to the latter.'

The second incident regarding the cemetery occurred some weeks later, but happened to be the first to come to my attention. The young man involved is now in the regular Army, but at the time he was employed by an associate of mine. Apparently he was a bit of an adventurer and not at all averse to a spot of ghost-hunting.

He was walking home with his girlfriend after having left a public house in Highgate. Their route took them down Swains Lane, past the eerie north gate of the graveyard. They were walking casually, hand-in-hand, when suddenly his girlfriend screamed at the top of her voice. Someone was standing behind the iron railings of the gate, just a few feet away as they walked by, and upon the face was an expression of terror.

They both stood petrified as the thing behind the gate appeared to dissolve into the shadows of the night.

On hearing about this from my associate, I managed to persuade the young man to take me to the place where the spectre appeared. There it stood, the rusting north gate, draped in barbed wire across the top of the corroding iron bars and permanently locked, refusing entrance even during the daylight hours. Behind the ominous north gate a path could be seen stretching between the mass of overgrown, lichen-covered gravestones. Deciding to look further into the matter, I arranged to meet the young man again the following week with a view to visiting the apparently haunted place at night. Meanwhile, I endeavoured to examine closely the cemetery itself and the history of the surrounding area.

It would appear that seven hundred years ago a castle dominated the place now called Highgate. It loomed three hundred and fifty feet above sea level, not far from London, and stood between two main roads which ran from the city. A large tract of country covering what is now Highgate Village to the Spaniards Inn and East Finchley to Muswell Hill was enclosed and used exclusively for hunting deer. By the sixteenth century the old castle was nothing more than a heap of rubble, overgrown with bushes and trenched with two deep ditches.

Highgate Cemetery itself was not opened until 1839, just six years after Highgate was made a parish. It soon became known as one of the most beautiful resting places in London. But not for long. By 1889 more than one hundred thousand bodies had been crammed into this tiny city of the dead. Over the years, that which was beautiful gave way to the grotesque hillside of ivy-covered Victorian vaults and uneven, jutting tombstones one now knows the cemetery to be. A sloping field of decay, the home of bats, owls and foxes, but mostly the home of human corpses.

This now dilapidated cemetery lies on a steep hill just a few minutes' walk from Highgate Village which distinguishes itself from surrounding districts by its curiously antiquated atmosphere somehow reminiscent of the seventeenth-century period when as a village it was considered to be quite important.

I decided to pay this eerie old place a visit. To reach the entrance I had to walk down the steep, winding Swains Lane which runs from the village and divides the cemetery into two quite distinct halves. The half at the top of the hill whose north gate one passes but cannot enter by, is decidedly in a greater state of decline than its counterpart further down on the left-hand side which contains the Karl Marx memorial. In this decomposing older part, however, the disused chapel, main gate and colonnade have been officially listed as historic buildings.

At the end of the tall brick wall flanking the western half of the cemetery I found the main gate and only entrance in use. Once past the massive iron gates I stood and surveyed my surroundings. Before me was a row of huge stone columns and to my left the old chapel in a state of considerable disrepair. Immediately, the curious atmosphere peculiar to this place and this place alone, enveloped me.

Narrow, melancholy paths ran in either direction; disappearing quickly into a forest of tombs. Straight ahead in the middle of the colonnade were stone steps leading to another path. These paths appeared eventually to meet at crossroads approximately in the centre of the western cemetery and continued on an upward journey through masses of graves covered and often hidden by weeds of every kind.

I discovered that, sooner or later, whichever path you take it will lead you to the large, pulsating heart of the cemetery - the Columbarium. This sunken circle of shadowy vaults and catacombs whose shelves occasionally spill.their mouldy contents as if gorged with too many coffins, was clearly the nucleus of the atmosphere which pervaded the graveyard. Some of the tombs had their entrances bricked up since the tranquility was disturbed by strange goings-on in past years. Well-worn steps reach into this dismal circle on both sides, but by far the most forbidding approach was a long Egyptian-style passage flanked by vaults on either side at the end of which a creaking, iron gate stood.

A fact which interested me was that the path from the disused north gate of the cemetery leads directly to the Columbarium: the path where the alleged phenomenon had been sighted. Feeling there were sufficient grounds to probe just a little further, I grew eager to meet the young man whose girlfriend had been frightened, and to pay a nocturnal visit. Little did I know that the meeting would never materialise.

A view of the Columbarium, showing a section of the outer-circle of vaults

On the night in question, the girlfriend appeared in his place and explained that on no account could her boyfriend be persuaded to go anywhere near the cemetery. I asked what had brought about this sudden change of heart and apparently the young man had taken it upon himself to go 'ghost-hunting' with a friend two nights earlier. So badly shaken was he by that experience that he did not want to duplicate it. His girlfriend also declined when I asked her to show me exactly how and where the spectre appeared. However, on the following day, I was able to question the young man about his 'ghost-hunting' activity and he told me the following:

> My friend and I arrived in Swains Lane shortly before midnight and scaled the wall (with some difficulty) close to the north gate. With our flashlights we followed the path into the cemetery for about a

hundred yards. To tell you the truth, I was intrigued by what I had thought was a ghost and the whole idea of searching it out seemed quite an adventure. In the back of my mind I don't think I really ever believed in such things and dark places, graveyards etc., have never bothered me.

Anyway, after a while both my friend and myself thought we heard a low vibrating noise - like a slow, booming sound - growing louder and louder. I say we thought because it seemed to prevail on other senses too. Like it could be felt...

Suddenly, a dark shape moved across the path directly in front of us. This is the only time we actually saw anything. No sooner was it there than it was gone. It is very difficult to describe the sickening feeling of fear which then surrounded us: the night air became heavy, very heavy. And our legs felt weak and trembled a great deal. For so reason I could think of at the time, or give you now, I recited the Lord's Prayer aloud. Shortly afterwards we regained strength and ran to the wall where we escaped.

Hope of visiting the cemetery with someone who claimed first-hand experience of the phenomenon being thwarted, I shelved the idea of probing further and concentrated on other matters. The Highgate mystery remained in its file for almost two and a half years untouched. Then, during the summer of 1969, I had a chance meeting with Elizabeth Wojdyla - one of the girls who had witnessed 'bodies rising from graves' in Highgate cemetery - and, seeing that she was anxious to speak to me, I invited her to have coffee at a nearby restaurant.

Although an intelligent and charming young lady, there was, nevertheless, a disturbing quality about Elizabeth. Her features had grown cadaverous and her skin was deathly pale. She appeared to be suffering from a pernicious form of anaemia. Her voice was faint and at times barely audible. She told me that she was working and had a flat where she lived on her own in the Highgate area. The thing that was troubling her was that the nightmares had returned. And returned with a vengeance. She gave me the following account of one such nightmare:

> Midnight had struck and I was slowly falling asleep. It is then that I experienced, not a dream, but something higher than that. I became aware of the stillness of the night and something approaching. Although I sense danger I cannot wake because I feel I am awake. All the time there is a feeling of something drawing closer and closer. I feel both hot and cold and am saturated with perspiration. Something is outside my window and I am filled with a mixture of fascination and terror. I am too drowsy, too weak to lift my head. My legs and arms feel as if weights have been attached to them. I cannot move.
>
> Suddenly, I become aware that whatever is approaching is at the foot of my bed. Then its form grows larger and larger. At first I think I see the face of a wild animal with glaring eyes and sharp teeth, but it is a man with the expression of an animal. The face is gaunt and grey. I feeL dizzy and grow faint. Something touches me. It feels icy cold. There is a strange, falling sensation and I remember no more.

These were all the details she could give me. I questioned her further, but realised that there was a void between us. She was prone to remaining silent for several minutes at a time, during which symptoms of the somnambulist were betrayed. Then, suddenly, life would return to her dark eyes and she would look up, smile, and continue as if nothing had happened. I managed to learn that she was also subject to headaches, dizziness, and, sometimes, nausea. A public place such as we were in made further discussion difficult, so I arranged to continue our talk the following evening at her flat.

The flatlet consisted of two large rooms and a kitchen, very sparse and without embellishment of any kind. Elizabeth greeted me and introduced me to her boyfriend, Keith, a tall young man of Scottish descent whose help was to prove invaluable. While Elizabeth made a drink, he told me more of her background: that she was of Southern Polish descent and brought up in a strict Catholic atmosphere. Her father was born in Krakow and was something of a disciplinarian; so much so that she found it difficult to remain under her parents' roof, and as Keith had not met with their approval, she had obtained a flat.

Elizabeth returned as Keith and I were chatting and remembered a strange experience when she first moved into the flat. She said: 'I was just sitting in front of the mirror, combing my hair to plait it for the night. Suddenly, the room felt much colder. For no apparent reason I became very frightened and aware of a humming noise in my ears. It seemed to grow louder. Then I thought there was someone standing behind me. I was too afraid to turn around. I just closed my eyes and "whitewashed" my mind. Eventually, it went away.'

I asked her whether she simply made her mind blank or concentrated on something in particular. Her reaction, she said, would have probably included a brief prayer, but she tried desperately to clear her mind.

She spoke of other incidents of a similar nature, including a number of occasions when she felt an urge to rise from her bed in the middle of the night and walk. It was as if she had to go somewhere, but where she did not know. I was preparing to leave, when Keith mentioned something about marks on the side of her neck. Elizabeth told him to stop being silly, that it was nothing. He remarked that they had been there for some time. As she was obviously reluctant about the matter I did not press to see what he was referring to and left.

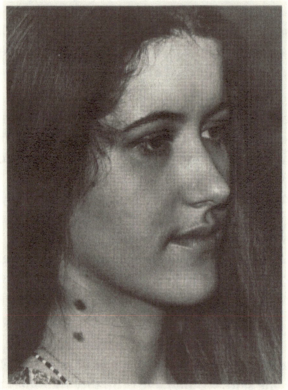

The 'mark of the vampire': two highly inflamed swellings on the neck of Elizabeth Wojdyla, a tiny hole in the centre of each

Some weeks later I received a telephone call from

Keith. He sounded anxious and asked whether he could see me as soon as possible. All he would say on the telephone was that it was about Elizabeth. I arranged to see him that same evening.

'Look, I'm sorry to bother you,' he began, 'but Elizabeth's condition has grown worse. She hardly eats and is so weak that she can hardly walk. And I'm afraid she is withering away at such a rate that she is barely alive. The doctor prescribes iron tablets and vitamin pills, but I think she needs help of a different kind. She is being overcome by something.'

I asked him what he meant by her 'being overcome' and his answer was that at times she appeared to be possessed by something dark and sinister. When asked if he believed in such things as 'possession' and 'demoniac molestation', he shrugged his shoulders, remained silent for a while, and then said that something was certainly possessing Elizabeth. I suggested that we visit Elizabeth immediately and on arrival I was taken aback by the marked deterioration in her appearance. She had lost a considerable amount of weight over the few weeks which had elapsed since I last saw her and her face was now dull and lifeless: the colour of marble.

She was extremely quiet and barely spoke all evening. As she sat, seemingly exhausted, in a large, comfortable chair, I noticed for the first time the marks on the side of her neck that Keith had referred to on a previous occasion. They were two inflamed mounds on the skin, the centre of each bearing a tiny hole. Elizabeth saw me staring and covered her neck with a scarf. I made an excuse to leave and Keith saw me to the door.

A picture of the Polish girl, Elizabeth Wojdyla, taken in her bedroom towards the end of the 'nightly visitations'

'What do you think?' he asked. 'Is it a case of possession?' 'It's too early for me to give a definite answer,' came my unsatisfactory reply. 'But I feel that Elizabeth should not be left alone in the flat at night. Could you stay with her and help her confront whatever is troubling her?'

'Yes, of course,' answered Keith. I told him that I would embark upon researching the area of possibilities which lay before us. He seemed immensely relieved to know that something positive was, at last, being done.

Three days later I received a letter from Keith. It read:

> On Wednesday evening I tried, as gently as possible, to confront Elizabeth with the notion that some force, of which her conscious mind is not aware or refuses to be aware, is controlling her actions for part of the time; in fact that the fight between the two forces is visible in her gestures and actions.
>
> Somewhere, very close to her conscious mind, she knows that something of this is true, but the full horror of the situation is too much for her to accept at the moment. The result is that she runs when anything nasty presents itself - this gives the dark side its chance to take over. On Wednesday, after this confrontation, she ran out into the night. I followed and eventually found her outside the gate of the cemetery at the top of Swains Lane.
>
> She was staring through the iron rails as if in a trance. Several moments passed, then, turning she walked back with me to the flat. I could see her flying from the thoughts I had presented to her, but my concern caused me to pursue the conversation even further. Suddenly, practically at the end of what I said, she announced that she had been trying to get out all evening (though in fact she hadn't). At this moment she became very upset, fraught: imprisoned is probably the best word to describe it. Moments later she changed and said it just seemed at the time as though I had been talking for ages.
>
> She can't face up to it yet, so she runs - a few moments after what is reported immediately above I tried to explain this to her and that she must try and face it or it will take her. She then ran and in the look she gave me I knew it had taken her: she was back in the trance again. Back at the flat, I slept on the couch in the room adjoining her bedroom. At about 1.00 am I was woken by a stifled cry coming from the direction of Elizabeth's room. I jumped to my feet and found her

> *gasping for breath, as if she had been almost suffocated. There were specks of blood on her pillow. I comforted her as best I could and remained there in her room till the daylight hours.*
>
> *How can she be helped? Should I encourage her to face up to it more and oppose whatever force threatens her? Please advise.*

That evening I made my way to the flat and was greeted by Keith.

'I arrived two hours ago. Been trying to get her to eat some broth I made, but she's hardly touched it,' he said.

'I must talk to you alone. Where is Elizabeth?' He noticed the grim note in my voice and replied that she was sleeping. 'You mention specks of blood appearing on her pillow in your letter,' I continued. 'How do you imagine they got there?'

'She probably coughed blood in her saliva when she was choking,' came his reply.

'Take a look at this,' I retorted, and handed him a photostat copy of an extract from *Dissertatio de Vampyris Serviensibus,* Duisburg, 1733.

He slowly read aloud the following translation:

> *They come out of graves in the night-time, rush upon people sleeping in their beds, suck out all their blood, and destroy them. They attack men, women, and children, sparing neither age nor sex. The people attacked by them complain of suffocation, and a great interception of spirit; after which, they soon expire.*

'I don't understand,' he said looking up. 'Who wrote this?' 'Professor Zopfius,' said I. 'One of the foremost eighteenth-century authorities on vampirism.'

'On what!' exclaimed Keith.

'Vampirism. Please read on.'

He continued:

> ...Some of them, being asked, at the point of death, what is the matter with them, say they suffer in the manner just related from people lately dead, or rather spectres of those people upon which, their bodies, from the description given of them, by the sick person, being dug out of graves, appear in all parts, as nostrils, cheeks, breast, mouth etc. turgid and full of blood. Their countenances are fresh and ruddy; and their nails, as well as hair, very much grown. And, though they have been much longer dead than many other bodies, which were perfectly putrefied, not the least mark of corruption is visible upon them. Those who are destroyed by them, after their death, become vampires; so that, to prevent so spreading an evil it is found requisite to drive a stake through the dead body, from whence, on this occasion, the blood flows as if the person was alive. Sometimes the body is dug out of the grave and burnt to ashes; upon which, all disturbances cease.

'But this is incredible,' Keith interjected. 'Are you saying that Elizabeth is in danger of becoming a vampire?'

'I am not saying anything at this stage. Let the facts speak for themselves and in doing so let us not overlook anything. We cannot dismiss the fact that Elizabeth is frequently disturbed by something in the night; that she is in some strange way attracted to Highgate Cemetery; that her anaemic condition is steadily worsening and that she bears tiny lacerations on her neck that in another age might be described as the "mark of the vampire".'

'But we're in this age and absolutely nobody will entertain the possibility of vampires,' Keith shouted.

'That is the very reason why we must. It is bound to be evaded by everyone else. Let us, at least, not make the mistake of overlooking it. Tell me, do you remember Elizabeth's room when she was living at her parent's house?'

He nodded.

'Well, can you remember if it contained any Christian symbols. A cross perhaps?'

'Yes, it did. In fact, the house was full of crucifixes and vessels containing holy water.'

'And here there are none. A little over two years ago Elizabeth was besieged by a series of "nightmares" almost identical to the ones she is having now, but they ceased. It might well be that a cross, the symbol of the triumph of good over evil, afforded her the necessary protection to keep the intruding malevolent force at bay. Of course when she moved here there was no longer any barrier.'

Keith wore an expression of amazement on his face. Then he quietly said. "She always used to wear a small, gold cross. She bathed and slept with it on, would never be without it. But she hasn't worn it for months.' Our eyes met and slowly shaking his head he added. "Can such things really be? Can they?'

I placed a hand on his shoulder to assure him. He looked bewildered. Then I said. 'Dare we risk ignoring a force whose strength lies in the fact that no one will believe it? If we are to help Elizabeth, we must act swiftly. If we are wrong it will do no harm. If we are right, there is no time to lose.'

'What must be done?' asked Keith.

'The door and window of her bedroom must be sealed with garlic and a crucifix. A handful of salt in a piece of linen must be hung round her neck together with a silver cross. Write the first fourteen verses of the Gospel according to St John and place the piece of paper beneath her pillow. Sprinkle the room liberally with holy water while repeating the Creed three times in a loud voice. Should she show signs of distress or anguish while she sleeps, it could well mean the force is nearby and trying to dominate her mind so that she will remove the impediments. At such times recite the following prayer: "Let us therefore most humbly pray to Almighty God that He would avert from this province and especially from this home every ill, and that He may be pleased to shield us from the innumerable crafts of Satan. From the snares of the devil, and from all pestilence, Good Lord deliver us." '

I left Keith with these instructions and the promise that I would return the following evening. When I did he had much to tell me.

'Last night I did as you asked and sat in an armchair in Elizabeth's bedroom. While she slept I watched as she writhed between the sheets as if fevered, emitting strange groans and gasps sporadically. Her forehead was burning and every so often her hands would search her throat for the cross you gave me to put there. I thought she would snap the chain on several occasions and gently returned her arms to her sides and comforted her as best I could. The cross around her neck definitely caused some consternation.

'Eventually I dropped asleep in the armchair, I don't know for how long, but suddenly I was awakened by a crash. A vase of flowers had been knocked over by the curtains and a howling wind blew in through the now open window. Elizabeth was sitting bolt upright in her bed and staring straight at the window. The cross was no longer around her neck.

'I sprang to my feet and made the sign of the cross, uttering the prayer you had given to me. Then I closed the window and went to Elizabeth who seemed unaware of everything that was happening. The cross, still on its broken chain, was on the floor by the bed. I replaced it on Elizabeth and resumed my guard. There were no further incidents.'

While Keith told me this, Elizabeth was in the kitchen preparing something to eat. After the meal, he kept her company in the living-room while I placed the ancient and approved vampire repellents about her bedroom. Keith was careful to keep the reason of our apparently unusual behaviour from her, lest she became unduly alarmed or think that we had gone completely crazy.

For about a week afterwards, Elizabeth was especially restless during her sleep and often requested the removal of the antidotes when she woke fevered and hot in the night. Sometimes Keith would discover one or two things had been disturbed by her during the day, but would always make sure that everything was in its proper place before dusk. Then, the endless nights of disturbed sleep subsided and Elizabeth returned to peaceful sleep. Her appetite was restored and the unhealthy, anaemic condition gave way to sparkling eyes and a glowing complexion once again. Keith bathed the small punctures on her neck with holy water until they faded and eventually disappeared. When Christmas came that year, she was her happy, normal self and all was well.

But one question haunted me: who else might be victim to the same devilish entity which preyed upon Elizabeth?

During the latter months of 1969 several colleagues of mine attempted a closer examination of the alleged phenomenon sighted by residents and passers-by in the proximity of High-gate Cemetery. The more they delved, the more people they discovered who had first-hand experiences of the 'Highgate ghost' as it was being called at the time. Tales of a mysterious, tall figure with a hideous countenance were almost legendary. Some witnesses were sufficiently disturbed to write to their local newspaper about it. This snowballed into a remarkable spate of reports at the commencement of 1970.

The following report appeared under the heading 'Ghostly walks in Highgate' on 6th February 1970, in the *Hampstead and Highgate Express:*

> Some nights I walk home past the gates of Highgate Cemetery. On three occasions I have seen what appeared to be a ghostlike figure inside the gates at the top of Swains Lane. The first occasion was on Christmas Eve. I saw a grey figure for a few seconds before it disappeared into the darkness. The second sighting, a week later, was also brief.
>
> Last week the figure appeared, only a few yards inside the gates. This time it was there long enough for me to see it much more clearly, and now I can think of no other explanation than this apparition being supernatural.

The following week's edition of the same newspaper was to include more confirmations of the 'ghost'. Here are just three extracts taken from three individual accounts that were published on 13th February 1970:

> My fiance and I spotted a most unusual form about a year ago. It just seemed to glide across the path. Although we waited a little while, it did not reappear. I am glad somebody else has spotted it: I was convinced it was not my imagination.

- A C, North Hill, Highgate

The ghost will sometimes appear nightly for about a week, and then not be seen again for perhaps a month. To my knowledge the ghost always takes the form of a pale figure and has been appearing for several years.

- K F, Mountbatten House, Hillcrest, Highgate

There is without a doubt a ghost. Of when and whom he originated I do not know. Many tales are told, however, about a tall man in a hat who walks across Swains Lane and just disappears through a wall into the cemetery. Local superstition also has it that the bells in the old disused chapel inside the cemetery toll mysteriously whenever he walks.

- R D, Highgate West Hill, N 6

In the following edition on 20th February 1970, of the *Hampstead and Highgate Express*, the editor himself wrote:

More readers confirmed this week that they have seen a ghost inside the gates of Highgate Cemetery.

But one of them, Mr Gerry Wood, of St John's Way, Archway, reported, I have waited with camera and transistor tape-recorder eagerly anticipating a ghostly apparition for two cold and bitter nights at that eerie place. All I have caught this far is a cold! But I shall persevere with camera at the ready - if only to prove the non-existence of the ghoul.'

There were to be many more disappointed free-lance ghost-hunters in the freezing weeks ahead. Meanwhile, in the same edition of 20th February 1970, the ghostly accounts continued:

A figure such as that seen by readers does haunt Highgate Cemetery. I caught sight of it while I was walking around the cemetery. I was on my way out - looking for the main gate. Suddenly, from the corner of my eye I saw something move, and immediately looked round to see a 'form' moving behind some gravestones.

My first reaction was that it was somebody 'mucking about' but looking back it seems strange that the thing made no sound and seemed to disappear into nowhere. I have been back a few times but have never seen it again.

- D W, Hillside Gardens, Highgate

The ghost startled a friend and myself when we were returning home from night duty. Being nurses we are able to deal with most situations, but the ghost, which seemed to be walking towards us from inside the gates, sent us running up Swains Lane as fast as we could.

- C S, Woodland Gardens, Muswell Hill

I am not at all surprised at the ghost experiences. I have also had a strange happening at the lower end of Swains Lane. A feeling of fear came over me and I started running with a hopeless thought I could not get away. When I turned to see if he was still there, the road was clear.

There was nobody in sight! Whoever or whatever it was, had vanished without trace. I am clear in my mind it was a ghost. My advice is to avoid Swains Lane during dark evenings if at all possible

- M F, Holly Lodge Mansions, Highgate

Although accounts of this terrifying spectre multiplied by the week, an extensive enquiry being made by certain colleagues of mine was enjoying little progress. Others, working in a freelance capacity, were likewise unable to shed any light on the mysterious phenomenon. Each probe ended up a totally blind alley. The strange case of the Highgate ghost' needed a fresh approach and the question which needed asking was: is it a ghost at all?

One thing which was uncovered by the considerable research being carried out at the time was evidence of the remains of a Satanic ceremony in the murky depths of the catacombs. This included pieces of burnt crucifixes, dried blood, splashes of black candle grease and traces of a curious mixture which when analysed turned out to be deadly nightshade, rue, myrtle covered in sulphur and alum, the majority of which had been burned.

At the beginning of 1970 I entered the investigation personally and gave it my undivided attention. From the start I was of the opinion that this spectre so frequently reported in the area of Swains Lane was no ordinary 'ghost'. In the first week of February 1970, a twenty-four-year-old man was knocked to the ground and attacked by something 'which seemed to glide' from the cemetery. He was much too shaken to write to the press, but it, nevertheless, came to my attention *via* someone he confided in. The description of a 'tall figure which swooped' down upon him with the countenance of 'a wild animal' was somehow not altogether unfamiliar. The appearance of a car with its headlights blazing down the lane caused the spectre to 'dissolve into the cemetery wall' and afforded the young man an opportunity to escape.

For a number of weeks, dead animals, notably nocturnal ones, kept appearing in Waterlow Park and Highgate Cemetery itself. Further inspection revealed that what they all had in common were lacerations around the throat and they were completely drained of blood.

As each piece of the uncanny puzzle was revealed I knew that here was a phenomenon that would certainly defy the mundane ghost-hunter's equipage of infra-red cameras and the like. Each failure of this supernatural being to be recorded by sophisticated means only served to confirm for me the true picture, albeit a picture of abject horror. It became appallingly apparent. The people of Highgate were not witnessing a harmless earth-bound apparition flitting across their graveyard, but a vampire!

The time had come to confront them with this revelation so that those already under the fatal malignity could be reached and helped. How many, I wondered, were keeping this undead nourished? The only way I could reach all the people in the area was to make public my opinion and some of the facts leading up to it. This I did with a certain amount of reluctance as most forms of publicity put investigations of this kind to considerable risk. However, as it was already a topic in the local press I felt that further harm would be minimal. More important was that those who recognised the symptoms would make contact. On Friday 27 February 1970, the front page headline of the *Hampstead and Highgate Express* read: 'Does A Wampyr Walk In Highgate?'

Among the many people who contacted me as a direct result of this public pronouncement was the sister of a beautiful twenty-two-year-old woman, whom I shall call Lusia. The initial letter expressed concern over her sister's unusual behaviour which included sleep-walking, something that she had never been prone to do in the past. Lusia also complained of being suffocated while she slept at night. Upon close examination her neck revealed two tiny pin-pricks that were far from noticeable. On two occasions she had left the flat whilst somnambulating and been found by her sister in Swains Lane walking towards the cemetery. I arranged for Lusia's sister to contact me by telephone immediately should Lusia leave her bed. The first two occasions she rang me late at night, I sped round to their flat, not a stone's throw from the cemetery, as quickly as I could and witnessed Lusia staring with a blank expression out of her bedroom window for about half an hour, then returning to her bed totally unaware of our presence. On the third occasion the telephone message had to be forwarded to where I was and there was some delay in my arrival. When I did arrive, shortly after midnight, there was a note on the door which read:

> *I did as you asked and left Lusia undisturbed. She peered out of her window for twenty minutes, but is now at the front door and undoing the locks. I shall stay with her. You know where she will be heading.*

I pushed the note into my pocket and ran as fast as I could up Swains Lane. There was no sign of either Lusia or her sister. I ran past the eerie north gate and into Pond Square. To my right was Highgate Village, to my left was Hampstead Heath. I chose left and within moments caught a glimpse of both young ladies entering the forecourt of St Michael's churchyard which backed onto Highgate Cemetery. Within a few seconds I had caught up with them.

There was Lusia, her face composed as if in a deep trance, slowly walking down the left side of the church with her sister several feet behind. Eventually she reached the back of the church's old broken railings, beyond which lay the cemetery. As Lusia passed through a gap in the railings and entered the graveyard, her sister grabbed my arm and pleaded that we take her home before she went any further. I consoled her as best I could, explaining how important it was that we discover the source that had drawn Lusia to this place.

That night we penetrated deep into the heart of Highgate Cemetery as we stumbled down stony steps towards the Columbarium. Fortunately, Lusia was wearing a white housecoat which was not too difficult to follow in the darkness which was illuminated only by the moon and stars. Nevertheless, we groped like the blind between great icy slabs of stone sinking in a sea of overgrown foliage. But, inevitably, Lusia led us to the catacombs. I knew that, at last, we were nearing our goal.

Lusia walked several yards round the Columbarium and then stopped before an enormous iron door. She stood silently for several minutes, facing the ominous entrance, then slowly raising her hands ripped the small crucifix which I had asked her sister to make sure she wore, from around her neck. Immediately I became aware of a low, booming vibration echoing through the catacombs. Her sister heard it too and became extremely frightened. Reaching into my coat pocket I produced a large silver cross and threw it so that it landed between the iron door and Lusia. At that moment, Lusia gasped and collapsed on the ground. We carried her home and put her to bed. The next day she remembered nothing of what had happened.

'Lusia' points to the spot where her sleep-walk ended
- before the large iron door which could not be opened
but beyond which lay three empty coffins

What was beyond the awesome door that drew Lusia to it in the dead of night? Could it be the unholy resting place of the undead which plagued Highgate? I made immediate plans for an official vampire-hunt!

Meanwhile, the headline of the *Hampstead and Highgate Express*, 6th March 1970, read: 'Why Do The Foxes Die?' The newspaper wrote:

> The mysterious death of foxes in Highgate Cemetery was this week linked with the theory that a ghost seen in the area might be a vampire.

Reports of the phenomenon from readers still continued to appear. The following was in the 6th March 1970 edition:

> One evening in January, my car broke down in Swains Lane. I pulled into the parking space by the cemetery gate. I am a practical person - even considered conservative - and things such as ghosts do not or did not, scare me. Suddenly, however, I noticed a terrible apparition gloating at me through the bars of the gate.
>
> Not being very brave I turned and ran - tripping head-first into a puddle and ruining my best suit. Scrambling to my feet I took a quick look over my shoulder, but to my great relief the 'thing' had gone. It never occurred to me it could have been a vampire, but if it was, then I consider myself lucky to be alive.
>
> - PF, Milton Park, Highgate, N6

Not all readers, however, supported a supernatural answer - much less the Vampire theory - as the following letter in the same edition shows:

> My interest in the Highgate ghost has been increasing in proportion to the number of ghosts unearthed. What a pity scientific investigation has killed the romantic supernatural quite dead, e.g., the United States Air Force has finally closed its books on the unidentified flying objects investigation and found our visitors from outer space had very earthy origins indeed.
>
> Swains Lane on a cloudy, windswept, moonlit night, with its cemetery, overhanging branches, sparsely-peopled, ill-lit, and rather Gothic, has the same effect on some people as reading a ghost story, and we all see ghosts after reading a ghost story. A strange moonlit shape, a moving shadow caused by car headlights, nocturnal animals moving about the graveyard, are all sources of ghostly visitants, incompletely observed and worked upon by a highly-charged imagination.
>
> Finally, with regard to the vampire theory. The British Occult Society is to be congratulated on fighting a brave last-ditch battle on behalf of the romantics in bringing their wampyr out of its dusty covers, and presenting it once again for public display, but alas, regretfully it is too late, by at least three generations
>
> - S L, Lisburne Road, Hampstead, NW3

The previous week's edition quoted the Rev. John Neil-Smith, Vicar of St Saviour's, Hampstead, saying: 'I believe the whole idea of vampires is probably a novelistic embellishment.' A curious comment, perhaps, for one of Britain's busiest exorcists to make. The following is a reader's reply in the 6th March edition:

> The Rev. John Neil-Smith says 'the whole idea of vampires is probably a novelistic embellishment.' It is this word 'probably' that I find disconcerting. It still leaves the question: 'Does a wampyr walk in Highgate?' A question that on the surface seems ludicrous, but, when you think about it, is no more fantastic than the supposition of a ghost or phantom that so many readers have amply attested to witnessing.

> One such reader asks 'must we exhume the ghost.' Well, if Mr Manchester's theory of a Vampire is correct, I would have thought the sooner it was exorcised the better. The question then remains, who would dare handle the job?
>
> - M M, Ufton Road, London N1

Who indeed, other than ourselves, could competently carry out the fearful task? I set the date for an official 'Vampire-hunt' on 13th March 1970, fully aware of the difficulties this undertaking presented. The *Hampstead and Highgate Express*; 27th February 1970, quoted me:

> We would like to exorcise the vampire by the traditional and approved manner - drive a stake through its heart with one blow just after dawn between Friday and Saturday, chop off the head with a gravedigger's shovel, and burn what remains. This is what the clergy did centuries ago. But we'd be breaking the law today.

As present-day law forbade us from disturbing the tranquillity of the tomb the only alternative was to await the undead's return to its coffin which would contain powerful vampire repellents and confront it before it took its cadaverous rest. This meant lying-in-wait during the dark hours and confronting the vampire before its supernatural powers subsided at dawn. The dangers were all too apparent, but we were left with little choice. Free-lance vampire-hunters were becoming a problem too. The *Hampstead and Highgate Express* published the following warning on behalf of the official investigation when one such individual made known his intention of taking on the vampire single-handed:

He goes against our explicit wish for his own safety. We feel he does not possess sufficient knowledge to exorcise successfully something as powerful or evil as this Vampire, and may well fall victim as a result. We also issue a similar warning to anyone with likewise intentions. (13th March 1970.)

During the second week of March, 1970, as the pending 'Vampire-hunt' drew closer, I was approached by Thames Television and asked to be interviewed at Highgate Cemetery for the 'Today' programme. I agreed.

The haunted icy path that runs from the North Gate to the Catacombs of Highgate cemetery. A member of the British Occult Society stands at the spot where the 'undead' figure has most often been seen.

The cemetery was covered in ice and snow as the 'Today' film team made its way to the north gate at the top of Swains Lane. Before filming commenced I took the interviewer, Sandra Harris, to the sinister catacombs of the Columbarium. It was bleak and bitterly cold. An eerie-sounding wind whistled through the icy, snow-covered vaults. She grew very uneasy and remained no longer than a few moments. The evil atmosphere had disturbed her sufficiently to eliminate her previous mood of jocularity. Eventually the cameras were ready and I prepared to be interviewed by the north gate where the spectre had been seen most often.

It was late afternoon and there was no sun on that grey, gloomy winter's day. Sandra Harris and I were one side of the old gate, while the camera crew were the other side. Sandra began by asking questions about the vampire. But something was wrong. There was a strange noise interfering with the sound said a technician. We tried again. But it was to no avail; the eerie noises only grew worse. Suddenly, the camera director fainted and fell to the ground. Then it seemed as if all hell broke loose. The wind literally howled and screamed through the trees; wires running from the generator van lashed the icy ground and Sandra's notes flew all over the place. The man who had collapsed was carried by members of the camera crew to a nearby van and rushed to hospital. Curiously, he had no previous history of fainting and no reason for this collapse was ever discovered. I asked Miss Harris whether she thought all this to be merely coincidental. She could not discount the possibility that it was not. Further attempts to shoot the interview by the north gate were abandoned and the actual interview took place outside the main gate further down Swains Lane.

Some independent witnesses, including a group of young children who had seen the spectre, were also interviewed for the programme. One said, 'Yes, I did feel that it was evil because the last time I actually saw its face and it looked like it had been dead for a long time.' Another witness commented, '...it seemed to float along the ground.'

The programme was screened at 6.00 pm on Friday, 13th March 1970: the eve of the proposed 'Vampire-hunt'. After hearing Eamonn Andrews promise a report on Highgate's vampire at the beginning of 'Today', viewers over an enormous area were acquainted with a present-day case of vampirism and the instruction: 'To exorcise a vampire one must first drive a stake with one blow through its heart, one should then chop off its head with a gravedigger's shovel, and then burn what remains.'

Two hours later, Highgate was the scene of utter pandemonium. From 8.00 pm onwards crowd upon crowd of onlookers flocked to Swains Lane. The number was to multiply again and again as car, van and bus loads continued to arrive from everywhere. A large number of police both on foot and in cars were unable to control the masses of people who by 10.00 pm resembled the size of a football crowd. All manner of free-lance vampire-hunters had appeared on the scene, including a history teacher, Mr Alan Blood, who had journeyed forty miles from Chelmsford, Essex, to seek out the undead being.

While the chaos and frenzy continued and, indeed, increased in Swains Lane, a group of one hundred persons led by myself, constituting the official vampire-hunt, made its way to the Columbarium in the inky darkness of Highgate Cemetery. The large iron door could not be opened. Try as we might, it would not budge an inch. I knew of another approach: a hole, just large enough for one person to squeeze through, in the roof of the elusive catacombs. It was quite a drop and I had to be lowered by a rope some twenty feet. Two assistants followed and we searched the musty, damp interior for signs of the undead's resting place, brushing aside cobwebs and items of decay as we went. In all we found three evacuated coffins which we proceeded to line with garlic and a cross. A circle of salt was poured around, and holy water sprinkled inside, each. Having done this we ascended the rope and rejoined those above.

Suddenly, the night-shrouded graveyard was pierced by thick white beams. The police were swinging searchlights over the cemetery as some of the crowd in Swains Lane had begun to spill over the locked gates and wall. I advised the main body of the vampire-hunt to return home at 12.45 am and remained in the vicinity of the tomb entrance with half a dozen hand-picked assistants. Shortly after 2.00 am the low booming vibration could be heard and felt. It was almost coming from beneath the ground itself. It grew louder and louder. Then it stopped. There was nothing more. We stayed there until sunrise -nothing appeared. I slipped back into the tomb: the coffins were just as I had left them. Empty.

Across the front page of the London *Evening News*, 14th March 1970, under the heading 'Satan Riddle Of Open Tomb', Londoners read:

> Nearly a hundred people joined in a vampire hunt at High-gate Cemetery today.
>
> Curious onlookers managed to scale the ten foot wall in search of an open tomb. Several people scrambled back frightened claiming they had seen 'something crawling' in the dark.
>
> Anthony Robinson, aged twenty-seven, of Ostel Road, Hampstead, came to the cemetery after hearing of the torchlight hunt.
>
> 'I walked past the place and heard a high-pitched noise, then I saw something grey moving slowly across the road. It terrified me.'
>
> 'First time I couldn't make it out, it looked eerie. I've never believed in anything like this, but now I'm sure there is something evil lurking in Highgate.'

The *Hampstead and Highgate Express*, 20th March 1970, had this to say:

> Police were called to control the crowd, which climbed the walls and rattled the gates.
>
> One of the watchers was Mr Alan Blood, twenty-five, a history teacher from Billericay. 'I have taken an interest in the black arts since boyhood, but I'm by no means an expert on vampires,' he said.
>
> 'Before investigating something like this I would get in touch with somebody more in the know.'
>
> 'Should such a thing exist, it could be very dangerous indeed.'

And still readers' reports of the phenomenon continued. The following appeared in the *Hampstead and Highgate Express*, 20th March 1970:

> *In July last year, on my way home from work about 9.30 pm I passed the cemetery while walking up Swains Lane. I had just recovered from a minor operation and on account of this had frequently suffered from short bouts of depression.*
>
> *On this particular night I stopped short at the sight of a figure running towards me without making any apparent noise. As soon as I realised this, I began to panic, but when I looked again the figure had disappeared.*
>
> *I know that many similar incidents have been related, but this may serve to confirm what has already been said.*
>
> - DO, Priory Close, Highgate, N6

The official investigation headed by myself continued, but there was no new evidence, no vital clues, to bring us closer to our goal. Then, four months later, something quite horrific happened. The *Hampstead and Highgate Express*, 7th August 1970 reported:

> *The discovery of a headless body and signs of a Satanic ceremony have renewed fears of a vampire cult centred around Highgate Cemetery.*
>
> *A police spokesman said: 'We are working on the theory that this may be connected with black magic. The body could well have been used for that reason.'*

The body, discovered by three fifteen-year-old schoolgirls, was lying on the grass outside a vault just a few yards from the spot where Lusia had led us in her sleepwalk. Here lay the key to the mystery - staring us in the face - yet we could not see it. I felt that it was time to re-examine the vaults of the Columbarium and their mouldy contents; not least of all the cavernous crypt which contained the three empty coffins. Lowering myself through the small opening in its roof, I once again descended the rope and looked for the coffins. Two were resting on the floor, exactly as I had left them with, perhaps, a few additional cobwebs. But one was missing.

Later that week I contacted Lusia to try and persuade her to accompany me on a daytime visit to the Columbarium. She reluctantly agreed and together with three assistants carrying the necessary accoutrements, we made our way on that August afternoon to the catacombs. Seating her comfortably twelve feet in front of the large iron door, I endeavoured to relax her as much as possible - she was of an extremely nervous disposition - and prepared to put her under a hypnotic trance. Eventually, after considerable inducement, she slipped deeper and deeper into trance. At first she answered questions in her normal voice, then, suddenly it changed and became deeper and more sinister. She kept saying, 'You should never have come here' over and over again. When I asked why, she replied, 'Evil has triumphed over good here.'

To further questioning she grew extremely distraught and I had to calm her. When she was settled I continued and tried to take her back to the night when her sleep-walking brought her to the place where we were now. After several attempts she began to re-enact that evening verbally, this time her normal voice had returned. When she got to the part where the somnambulism began, all she would say was, 'Yes, yes, I'm coming...' I asked her where she was going and who was calling her. A smile flickered across her face and she repeated, 'I'm coming.'

Then she started laughing and, suddenly, stood up and cried out, 'Where are you?' several times. I instructed my assistants to keep well back and not restrain her. She ran to the iron door and grabbing its rails screamed 'Where are you?' yet again. It echoed through the catacombs. Then, turning, she slowly walked to a vault entrance nearby and began sobbing. It was the vault outside which the headless corpse had been discovered. I consoled Lusia and carefully brought her out of the trance.

Could this be it, I wondered, staring at the heavy iron doors of the vault. Was I on the point of realising the goal of my mysterious investigations? The answer waited behind those rusty doors. Had I discovered the resting-place of the undead where the empty coffins were and was this now a new resting-place since I had disturbed the old one? There was no time to lose, for if this was the place it would cease to be so very much longer, now that I had found it. Last time, night was on the undead's side; this time I was afforded a most welcome ally: daylight. We all put our shoulders to the old doors and slowly inch by inch, they creaked open until we were able to gain entry.

Inside it was dark and the most awful stench assailed our nostrils. The shelves were full of decaying coffins. I began counting them and after checking with the number of inscriptions outside, there appeared to be one too many. But which one? Then I realised that the one on the floor at the very back of the vault was in much better condition than the rest and bore no nameplate. We approached it very cautiously and, with hearts pounding, raised the lid.

There it lay: a body which appeared neither dead nor alive. Eerily, we gazed at that sight which defied explanation and logic for several long moments. 'It's newly dead,' said one of my assistants, breaking the silence. But the vault was a hundred years old and there had been no recent admissions. As he spoke. I took up a stake made of aspen and placed the point between the seventh and eighth rib on the left. Grabbing my arm the same assistant pleaded with me to desist saying that it would be sacrilege. If what lies before us is an undead, I replied, it would be an act of healing. Consternation grew among the group in the vault and the consensus of opinion was that the stake remained unsoiled until, at least, proper permission had been obtained from the correct quarter. I tried to explain that such permission would almost certainly be refused and that, anyway, by then it would be too late. 'Is there no other way?' asked an assistant. 'We can try,' I said, 'we can try.'

We had to act quickly for the sun would soon be setting. Replacing the lid of the coffin, I rested a crucifix upon it and placed vessels containing holy water at the four corners. Bags of salt and garlic were placed strategically inside the vault and incense was burned at the entrance. We retreated to the doorway and outside I prepared a circle of salt inside of which we all stood. Handing a crucifix to each of the participants I requested that they all pray in silence for a few moments, asking for strength and support to banish this thing of evil for ever. I explained to Lusia that during the ensuing ceremony she must remain inside the circle and do exactly as instructed. I gave her a Bible to hold open at the fifty-fourth Psalm.

After a brief pause, I began the ancient exorcism, sprinkling holy water and making the sign of the cross between each prayer of invocation, each plea for strength, and all the adjurations.

> O Thou Who dost answer the prayers of Thy humble servants, strengthen these efforts in Thy name to counteract the subtleties and evil mischiefs of him who is the Devil's agent. Cause the forces of darkness to be overcome by the angels of light, for the sake of Jesus Christ our Lord.

As I began the Latin banishment, it suddenly grew very cold and the white candles burning round the circle flickered as if something had caused a draught. One of my assistants placed a hand upon my shoulder and pointed skywards. The sun was setting. I continued with added fervour and now shouted the words of the exorcism so that they reverberated off the walls of the vault:

> Go forth thou deceiver, full of all evil and falsehood, the enemy of virtue, the persecutor of the innocent. Give place thou wicked one; give place thou evil one; give place to Christ.

Instantaneously, those deep, voluminous, booming sounds began vibrating through the tombs. Lusia became extremely frightened and dropped the Bible she was holding. An assistant grabbed her just as she was about to step out of the circle. Dusk was upon us. Raising my right hand which held a large crucifix I cried: 'Begone, thou hideous demon, unto thine own place and return no more to plague the children of Almighty God.'

Then I threw the cross with all my might into the darkness of the vault. Only silence followed. We stood surrounded by that stony silence for a long while, not daring to move. Then I said that it was over and we prepared to leave. Picking up the Bible which Lusia had dropped, I noticed that it had fallen open at Deuteronomy. My eyes ran across the words: 'Only be sure that thou eat not the blood: for the blood is the life...' - chapter 12, verse 23.

Sean Manchester at the vault where the suspected undead was eventually located. A picture taken just prior to the exorcism ceremony

Upon our recommendation the entrance to the vault was bricked and cemented up.

The exorcised vault after the ceremony, bricked up and permanently sealed. Garlic was included in the cement mixture and a crucifix hung behind the doors that will never see daylight again.

The following appeared in the *Hornsey Journal* on 28th August 1970, under the heading, 'Secret Exorcism At Highgate Tomb':

> *Seven crucifixes, four white candles, and four cups of holy water from a Catholic Church, were used in the fifteen-minute ceremony. It was carried out by four men and a woman who met on an August afternoon near the entrance of a vault where a headless woman's corpse had been found.*
>
> *Incense was burned and holy water was sprinkled near the vault,*

and the banishment of evil powers, including words in Greek, Latin, Hebrew and English, was read by Mr Sean Manchester, president of the British Occult Society.

A documentary reconstruction of the exorcism was made for BBC television and selected portions were shown on the BBC's programme 'Twenty Four Hours' in October 1970.

News of the exorcism ceremony brought a sigh of relief to many living in the Highgate area and a good many more considered it to be the final chapter of the Highgate Vampire. As far as the British Occult Society is concerned, the file must remain open. We might have come face to face with the vampire, but there is, too, the uncertainty that even if we had, evidence of its destruction is far from conclusive. The stake was not struck!

Strange occurrences, moreover, have failed to cease. In the same week that the exorcism took place, a man was found covered in blood in Highgate Cemetery. He died in hospital ten days later. The blood had poured from a throat wound according to official sources.

That the malign supernatural might still hold sway in this eerie Victorian graveyard cannot be discounted. Over its one hundred and thirty odd, very odd, years, Highgate Cemetery has kept its secrets well. Mention its name, however, to anyone who knows the place and their reply will almost certainly be, 'Oh yes, Highgate Cemetery, that's the place where the vampire is.' For this place which owes its fame not to the dead who lie still in their bony dust, but the ones who do not, has become synonymous with vampirism. The owners have now, quite understandably, closed the western cemetery to the public. The catacombs can no longer be visited and enjoy a long-wished-for privacy uninterrupted by prying humans. Whether or not the undead still rises from the bricked-up vault when the sun disappears and night falls is a question which must, for the time being, remain unanswered.

Like the miracles of dead saints, recorded cases of vampirism are not plentiful in this day and age. This could quite easily be attributed to the fact that while we have succeeded in exploring the continents of our planet and, indeed, put men on the moon, we have scarcely begun to explore the whole vast world of the supernatural. Blinded by science, we conveniently explain away paranormal phenomena or tuck them comfortably under the headings of fantasy and fiction. Until, that is, they unearth themselves as they did in Highgate with the resulting head-on confrontation. On that occasion, the door between us and another world was almost ripped off its hinges.

The purpose of this account has not been an attempt to vindicate the reality of the vampire, nor is it a treatise on the subject, but rather a report of a series of events which actually took place in twentieth-century England.

FOUR NEW VAMPIRE STORIES

DOMDANIEL

by Peter Allan

[PETER ALLAN is the pseudonym of a well known writer and broadcaster who lives in an isolated and eerie old house buried in the countryside of England. Long interested in folklore and legend, vampires in particular have fascinated him ever since he read Dracula and saw the Bela Lugosi film as a boy. He has no doubt that vampires of a kind once existed or that they may still be found if one knows where to look...]

['Domdaniel' is based on a true experience...]

'Never shall I forget the scene that met my eyes when I walked into the Long Room...'

It takes a long time to reconcile oneself to living in a foreign country but for years now I have almost regarded myself as an Englishman; in reality I am one of those fortunate refugees who escaped from Eastern Europe when the troubles began there some thirty years ago, and I have never been back.

The years have passed peacefully enough and I have become so settled that I have never been sufficiently interested to establish whether or not I still have any relatives alive on the continent. It is unlikely, and long ago I settled in to the life of the English.

I have spoken English for so long that I now look upon it as my native tongue - well, almost anyway. I married an English girl soon after I came here and two lovely daughters completed our family.

I have become fascinated by the English and over the years I have spent hours of enjoyment at my desk, poring over volumes of ancient legend, folklore and myth for the various superstitions, odd customs and strange beliefs of the inhabitants of these islands. This has become an absorbing interest with me and I never miss an opportunity to note down local legends whenever I visit any part of Britain. Often, I fear, I have driven my family almost to distraction when they would have much preferred we drive on past some dreary little church and village, to a larger town with shops. But they have respected my interests and even on our holidays they have become accustomed to our route invariably wandering here and there to visit some obscure mound, stone circle or ancient burial place, some old building or reputed site of some long-forgotten event.

They were not surprised therefore, after we decided on a touring holiday in Scotland, to find that I had devised a route that bypassed most of the towns! However, we compromised; little thinking that we were to find ourselves in the middle of an adventure so strange that in writing it down it sounds more like fiction than fact. Yet it happened; yes, it's all only too true...

After visiting the Lake District on our way north from the outskirts of Oxford where we had lived for the past fifteen years, we made our way towards Edinburgh, our ancient black Ford only grumbling occasionally at the steepest hill. It was evening when we approached Edinburgh and since none of us had visited the city before, we decided to spend the night outside and enter and explore by daylight after a night's rest.

We noticed a sign advertising accommodation and succeeded in obtaining an evening meal and bed and breakfast for ourselves at a farmhouse where the friendly but cautious inhabitant fed us well. In the morning we set off in sunshine, refreshed and excited at the prospect of exploring Scotland's finest city.

I had read a lot about the legends and stories of strange happenings that abound in Edinburgh and while my wife and my daughters, Joan and Julia, went window-shopping, I explored the older parts of the city. I found the Museum of Antiquities with its Treasure of Traprain: that collection of church plate discovered in a crushed and broken condition after a raid into Gaul in the fifth century; the Cinerary urns; the flag carried by Douglas at the Battle of Otterburn in 1388; the strange stones carved with peculiar designs that no one has succeeded in interpreting; the seventeenth-century thumbscrews and manacles; the guillotine by which so many notables lost their heads. I visited too the curious stone graves at the corner of Castle Hill; Brodie's Close, the habitat of Brodie, a reputable citizen by day and burglar by night who was eventually hanged by a drop improved by himself; the Witches' Walk haunted by the ghost of Robert Louis Stevenson - and the hours flew by and it was time to meet my family and resume our journey into Scotland.

We had intended to make our way up the east side (taking in a visit to historic Glamis Castle with its ghosts and rooms of mystery), crossing somewhere in the vicinity of Loch Ness, hoping to catch a glimpse of the legendary monster, and then make our way back down the west coast with visits to some of the Western Isles; but a few hours after we left Edinburgh the weather changed so we turned off west in the hope of leaving the bad weather behind us.

Having the best part of a fortnight before us we were

not worried by the fact that as I turned first southwards lighter skies and north towards a break in the lowering clouds, we had virtually no idea of where we were.

It was now late afternoon and in appalling weather we topped the crest of a hill in a heavily-wooded stretch of countryside and were relieved to see far below a few houses clustered together around a winding river. By some freak of nature a shaft of sunlight from the setting sun covered the little community, sheltering at the foot of the hills - mountains almost - on every side and we decided that we would see whether we could put up there for the night.

Several times we lost sight of the hamlet for the rain lashed against the windscreen of the car and now and again we would encounter what seemed to be banks of fog. Twice we almost gave up and decided to turn back but then one or other of us would catch sight of the village again and off we would go, slipping and slithering along the pitted and narrow road that twisted and turned ahead of us in the failing light.

Oddly enough each time we saw the village, it seemed just as far away as when we had first seen it and that was hours earlier. Then suddenly, after none of us had seen anything but the blinding rain lashing the trees and hedges bordering the road, until we expected at any moment to find our path blocked by a fallen tree, we seemed to pass out of the storm into a calmness that had an unreal quality after the fury of the rain.

We found ourselves among the houses that we had seen from afar.

Now that we were close at hand we could see in the gathering dusk that the houses were very old indeed. As we slowly made our way past the silent, shadow-ridden cottages, we saw no trace of life other than the lighted windows that told us there were in fact inhabitants in this seemingly deserted place.

We had passed perhaps half a dozen houses when I decided that we ought to see whether we could find accommodation so I stopped the car, told my family to wait, and approached the stone doorway of the nearest cottage.

There was still just enough light to make out the stout wooden door set in the deep walls of the cottage. I noticed a niche above the doorway and could dimly make out a figure of some kind set into the stone.

Inside the cottage I could hear the sound of muffled speech and I banged on the door with my fist for I could see no knocker. Immediately there was complete silence. I waited a moment and when there was still no sound, I knocked again. Again only silence answered me.

I knocked a third time and called out 'Is anyone there?' I heard more muffled talking and the sound of someone shuffling towards the door so I stood back and waited.

Although I judged the occupant must have reached the door no effort was made to open it, so I knocked yet again and called out, 'Is anyone there? I've lost my way.'

I heard the sound of a bolt being withdrawn and a heavy latch being lifted. The door creaked open a few inches and I saw half a face, including one wide-open eye, a shock of red hair and a ragged red beard silhouetted against a dimly-lit interior.

'I'm sorry to trouble you,' I explained. 'But I seem to have lost my way and as it is getting dark I wondered whether you might know where my family and I could stop for the night?'

'No - no room,' replied the man. 'Best move on - move on...! and the door was shut in my face and I heard the latch fastened and the bolt shot home.

I turned and made for the next cottage, about fifty yards away. As I passed the window of the cottage I had knocked at, I noticed several faces pressed against the windowpane, watching me. As I walked towards the second dark and squat dwelling in that silent hamlet I again noticed a stone figure set in a niche above the doorway and I made a mental note to find out the reason for those odd appendages; something I had never seen before in Britain.

The reaction to my arrival at the second cottage was almost identical to my original experience. At my initial knock the murmur of voices within ceased abruptly. At the second knock I heard footsteps approach the door followed by more silence and on my third knock I heard bolts withdrawn. The latch was lifted and the door was carefully opened a few inches to reveal the apprehensive face of a wiry and elderly Scot who looked at me enquiringly without saying a word.

I smiled and said as pleasantly as I could that I seemed to be lost and wondered whether there was any chance of finding accommodation for my family and myself for the night. This time I was not even rewarded by a word of refusal. Only a curt shake of the head before the door was closed and the bolts shot home.

I returned to the car and, having related my experiences, decided to proceed a little further and see whether I could find a less inhospitable inhabitant. I was on the point of suggesting that we press on through the village until we reached somewhere else but my wife and daughters looked so exhausted after the tiring journey through the storm that I decided to try and find somewhere to stop as soon as possible.

We passed a few more cottages, none of which looked more inviting than those I had already tried, and then we came upon a corner house, a little larger than most of the cottages we had seen so far, and there the door was open and someone was standing with his back to the road reaching up over the door. I quickly pulled up but by the time I was out of the car the person had disappeared and the door was shut.

I hastened up the little path and knocked at the door. All was quiet within. I knocked again and almost immediately the door was opened. The man who now faced me must have been standing just inside. He was a big man, dressed iri a collarless striped shirt and thick working trousers. Although he looked as though he would be a match in strength for any two ordinary men of my size, he seemed nervous and looked anxiously at me and beyond me to the car containing my family.

I'm terribly sorry to trouble you,' I began. 'But I seem to have lost my way. My family are fatigued and I wonder whether you could possibly suggest where we might find accommodation just for the night?'

As I spoke the man had been surveying me from head to toe. His glance returned to my face. 'Come far?' he asked, almost rudely.

I was grateful to receive any answer. 'Oh, we're touring,' I said hurriedly. 'But there was a storm and we lost our way. We'd be so grateful for a night's lodging. We'd be off first thing in the morning. Can you possibly help? I have money,' I added, pulling out my wallet.

The man looked at the money and then back at my face. He seemed to be trying to decide whether I could be trusted. After a moment he evidently made up his mind.

'Sorry - no room...' and he made to close the door. 'Oh, I see,' I spoke hurriedly again, before the door closed completely. 'That's alright... er ... could you suggest where I might be more fortunate? Is there an inn here, or a big house where you think they might have room?'

The man stood looking at me through the half-closed door. 'The big house...' he said slowly, a waver in his voice. 'The big house...' he said again slowly. 'Yes, they've got room, but I don't think...' he seemed at a loss for words. 'Try the inn, The Full Moon, round the corner there but I don't know, I don't know... why don't you go on through the pass...?' And the door closed.

As I turned to go something touched my head and looking up I saw yet another niche over the doorway. This time the light from our car headlamps gave me a better view and I saw that the stone figure set in the niche seemed to be a male figure in a hood carrying a stake in one hand and a curious and inappropriately large cross in the other. Hanging from the figure I saw a bunch of leaves that the occupant had evidently been putting in place when I had arrived and this was what had brushed my head. I looked closely and was surprised to find the narrow leaves and ball of flowers that I had often seen growing wild in Southern Europe. It was garlic.

I was puzzled for a moment; but the plight of my family, anxiously peering at me from the interior of the car reminded me that it was accommodation we were looking for and I hastened to tell them there was an inn nearby.

The Full Moon looked deserted when we eventually found it. I could see no lights at all but when I reached the door, I found it opened at my touch and I stepped inside. The sound of talking that had reached my ears as I opened the door ceased abruptly as I entered and I found myself being surveyed with something more than idle curiosity by the landlord, leaning on the bar, and half a dozen or so occupants, dotted about the sparsely-furnished room.

I nodded to the men staring at me silently over their drinks and walked towards the bar. The innkeeper gave no smile of welcome and gazed steadfastly at me.

'Good evening,' I began. 'Could I have a pint of bitter, please?' The innkeeper took a glass and filled it, still keeping his eyes fixed upon me. I put my money on the bar and took the glass. After a long drink I replaced the half-empty glass on the bar and smiled at the landlord. He seemed more relaxed now and actually nodded at me.

'Lovely countryside hereabouts,' I ventured, by way of an opening. 'We're touring and seem to have lost our way.' The landlord made no comment and I thought it best to continue. 'Actually, we were wondering whether you could accommodate us for a night - then we can be on our way first thing in the morning;' I added hurriedly as I saw him begin to shake his head.

'No room,' he said at last, after what seemed an age of pregnant silence. 'I'd get on if I were you.'

'Yes, well,' I began again. 'My wife is very tired and we've come a fair way. We'd like to stop here just for the night, if we could. Anywhere would do, just for the night. Couldn't you possibly find somewhere ... I'd be most grateful,' I added, pulling out my wallet.

'No - no - no room at all here,' the innkeeper replied, almost too quickly.

I took another drink as he spoke, waiting for him to suggest an alternative. When he said no more I put the empty glass down and asked: 'Well, what about the big house - do you think they might take us for one night?'

The landlord started visibly. 'The big house - oh, I wouldn't think so. No, I'd not recommend that!' I was beginning to feel that I was taking part in a film; it all seemed so unreasonable, so unreal and so unwelcoming.

'I say, but look here,' I said with a little more spirit. 'We're visitors and surely there must be somewhere we can stop for a night. We seem to be miles from anywhere and we need to rest before going on. If you're sure you can't help us, tell me the way to the big house and I'll try there.'

The innkeeper thought for a moment. He looked at the others in the room. 'He's away, isn't he?' he asked, of no one in particular. I looked round at the nearest couple of men but they sat silent with their drinks in front of them. Then both gave a brief nod to the landlord, whereupon he turned back to me.

'Well, try the big house if you like. You'll find the drive a quarter of a mile along the road here, on your left. The gate will be fastened so you'll have to leave your car and walk up to the house. Old Henrock will be there, but don't say I sent you

He turned abruptly and went to the other end of the bar and began to fill a glass for himself. 'Thank you,' I said, turning to go. 'And goodnight,' I received no reply and made my way out of the inn.

By this time my wife and daughters were beginning to be tired of my repeatedly saying that I could find no sympathy wherever I called, in what I was beginning to think must be the most unwelcoming village in Scotland, and when I said that I was going to try the big house as a last resort, my wife insisted that she would accompany me and see whether she could persuade 'old Henrock' to take us in for the night.

By now it was quite dark and my wife and I climbed over the gate - there was no other way for us to enter for the massive gate was fastened with a heavy chain wound several times round the gate and gatepost before being locked with a padlock that looked rusted as if it had been unused for years.

As we made our way along the overgrown drive the wind rose and we found ourselves labouring against great gusts of wind that blew the low-hanging branches of the mass of trees bordering the drive, into our faces. We pressed on to the accompaniment of occasional hootings of owls and swirling bats that frightened the life out of my wife who was afraid, like so many women, that they would get caught in her hair. Now and again we caught sight of the dark outline of a house ahead of us and, to our relief, we saw a light in one of the upper windows.

We were about twenty yards from the door, set in a massive arch with wide steps leading to it, when we realised that the door was open and as we drew nearer we could distinguish someone standing in the deep shadow of the doorway. Hand in hand we hurried across the last few yards and into the doorway out of the driving wind and swirling leaves.

'Sorry to trouble you...' I began. The figure of a man, tall and forbidding in the dim light, detached itself from the shadows and stood looking down at us. He was dressed in black or very dark clothing, unrelieved even by a white shirt for he wore a dark high-necked sweater under a black velvet jacket. By contrast his face, clean-shaven and unwrinkled although he was certainly not a young man, was almost chalk-white. His piercing dark eyes flashed from my face to that of my wife, and stayed there. Hardly moving his lips he said in a faraway voice with a foreign accent, 'How did you get in? What do you want? This is private property. The master is away.'

I put an arm around my wife's waist and we pressed towards the doorway. May we come in for a moment, please? We've lost our way and seeing the drive, we climbed over the gate in the hope that someone could help us.'

Henrock, for he it was we later learned, stood to one side and with a theatrical gesture, bade us enter. Doing so we found ourselves in a large hall with an enormous sweeping staircase ahead of us. So much we could make out in the dim light before we heard the door crash to behind us and, startled for a moment, we turned to find Henrock bolting and chaining the heavy door before turning and striking a match. He passed us and lit two candles that were mounted one each side of the staircase in wrought-iron holders decorated with dragons' heads. He placed himself carefully just behind one candle and looked down on us.

'The master is away,' he said again as if that statement would answer all our problems.

'Yes...' I said, unable to think of the best line of approach. My wife came to my rescue. Brushing her long hair back from her face, she faced him with her most attractive smile and said, demurely: 'We *are* sorry to trouble you but we are at our wits' end. We've been lost for ages and just can't go any further. If you could possibly see your way to allowing us to spend the night here, we'll be extremely grateful and we promise to be no trouble at all. We really are tired out. We'll gladly recompense you for your kindness and we'll be away first thing in the morning. Please...' she hesitated to allow full emphasis to her words. 'Please - we'd be so grateful.'

Henrock hadn't taken his eyes from my wife's face as she spoke and now he answered, still staring at her. 'The master is away.' he said yet again. 'I don't know when he will be back. He is not accustomed to visitors. We have no food.' He hesitated for a moment and my wife, pressing her advantage, pleaded: 'Please, oh, please, just let us rest until the morning

Henrock said nothing for a moment, half-smiled, revealing two appallingly ugly upper side teeth, and then he abruptly turned and walked away from us up the stairs. 'Follow me,' he called over his shoulder.

With a glance of relief at each other we followed him up the stairway and into a room where candles were burning in a low-slung chandelier. He indicated that we should enter and pointed to a wooden seat by the window. Taking up a position with his back to the door he said, hesitatingly: 'I don't know whether the master would approve, but stay the night in this room if you wish; now I will leave you,' and he was almost gone before I called out: 'Oh, our daughters are in the car at the end of the drive. Do you think you could unlock the gate so that we can bring the car up to the house?'

Henrock turned, his dark eyes flashing for a moment. 'You said nothing of any children?' 'Er - well, no...' my wife interjected. 'We were just going to say that we hoped you would extend your hospitality to them. They are not children, actually, they're nearly twenty. They won't be any trouble though - they just need somewhere to sleep. You don't mind, do you?'

Henrock stood silent for what must have been the best part of a minute. 'They can sleep in the master's room,' he said at last. 'But I can't open the drive gates,' he added quickly. 'You must leave the car where it is. It will be quite safe,' he added. 'No one comes here.' The next moment he was gone.

I looked at my wife. 'Stay here; I'll fetch the girls and lock the car,' I told her. 'I'll bring the little suitcase. We'll be off early in the morning...' When I was halfway down the staircase I heard a door open behind me and Henrock appeared carrying a candle in a long brass holder. He stood in the doorway of the room at the head of the stairs. 'This is the master's room,' he said in a reverend tone. 'I'll leave the door open.' I was about to answer when I realised that he had gone.

Half an hour later we had said 'goodnight' to the girls and they were in their room. We prepared ourselves for the night and before long were thankfully tucked up, close together for comfort, in the brass bedstead in the corner of the room, having extinguished the candles.

There were no curtains to the windows and for a while we lay awake, thinking our own thoughts, and watching the clouds scurry across the moonlit sky.

We both awakened with a start as a clap of thunder seemed to shake the house. The storm we had travelled through seemed to have reached the village and lightning streaked across the sky lighting up our shadowy room; the wind howled; the uncurtained window rattled and shook as it was beaten by gusts of wind, the pouring rain, and what looked like branches; and for some time we were unable to get back to sleep. At length the storm passed and we resumed our rest - only to wake again with sickening suddenness at the sound of a piercing shriek - Joan's voice!

I leapt from the bed and pulled at the door. It was shut fast and seemed to be locked! I shouted, I banged at the door. I shouted and kicked but all to no avail. All was now quiet and in fact there were no more screams after that first awful one. I listened intently but could hear no sound whatever. The house might have been empty. I tried the door again for one last time but it was closed fast and nothing I could do would shift it. There was nothing for it but to go back to bed and wait for morning.

We tossed and turned for some hours until I could stand it no longer. I looked at my watch and saw to my astonishment that it was barely three o'clock, but I knew that I should not sleep any more. My wife too was wide awake. 'I'm going to get up,' I said. I looked out of the window. It was still dark.

I began to get dressed when suddenly the door of the bedroom opened and Henrock stood there. He was dressed exactly as we had seen him the previous night but he seemed agitated.

'The master returned last night,' he said simply. 'As your daughters have his room he is downstairs. I think you had all better leave as soon as you can.' I was about to question him about the fastened door and the scream, but he had gone. 'I'll see about the girls,' I said to my wife. 'Get dressed quickly.' I ran out of the room and saw Henrock turn the handle of the master's room; he just opened the door, closed it again and then went downstairs.

I dashed into the room occupied by our daughters. They were awake and looked wide-eyed at my sudden entry. 'Are you alright?' I enquired, breathlessly. 'Henrock says his master has returned and we must leave. Get dressed as quickly as you can and we'll be on our way. Oh, and what was that scream in the night?'

'Oh!, my God!, what a night,' replied Julia. Joan had a nightmare or something and nearly frightened the life out of me. We'll tell you all about it later. Hey, come on Joan, you look awful - it was only a dream after all...'

Shortly afterwards we all gathered at the head of the stairs with our belongings. Joan did look pale and she seemed quite weak but her mother said it was all the travelling and the disturbed night, so I did not take too much notice.

We made our way down the stairs and had reached the door without seeing anyone when I caught sight of Henrock standing in the shadow of a doorway leading off the hall. He didn't move out of the shadows as he spoke.

'Ah! we're just off,' I said. 'Please accept this for your trouble.' I handed him the ten pound note I had ready. 'We were grateful for the night's shelter. I do hope your master was not too inconvenienced by our being here?'

Henrock still did not move and he made no attempt to take the money. 'The master wishes to see you,' he said flatly and opening a door behind him he stood to one side. I took a step towards him while my wife and daughters remained by the front door. 'All of you,' Henrock added, and directed us inside the room.

With some trepidation we walked together into the room. It was as sparsely furnished as the rest of the house that we had seen but seated at a grand piano was a man whose appearance defies an adequate description.

I never saw anyone like him before. He seemed old yet there was a sprightliness and magnetism about him that belied the long white hair and the scraggy neck for his face was unlined and full, bloated even. His dark eyes were overshadowed by bushy black eyebrows that looked like tufts of feathers, eyebrows that seemed to run from one side of his face to the other. He looked intently at each of us and then his eyes returned with piercing intensity to the girls. Suddenly he seemed to remember his manners and he turned to my wife and me with a charming old-world courtesy, rising from the piano with outstretched hand.

'Welcome to Domdaniel', he said in a deep voice, almost without moving his lips, much as Henrock had spoken, and I remembered wondering whether this was a family idiosyncracy and whether Henrock and his master were related for there was a similar bearing and sense of dignity about both of them - yet this seemed most unlikely; and the master was if anything even taller than the servant.

'Welcome to Domdanier he said again, indicating a long seat by the window, which was uncurtained, although it was still dark outside. 'Forgive me,' he went on. 'I was forgetting, it is dark in here.' And he lit a candle on the piano. 'I'm afraid I enjoy the dark,' he said, with a ghost of a smile. Having lit the candle he came towards me with outstretched hand. 'My name is Domain, Damon Domain and I apologise for my inadequate hospitality. I have long ago forgotten the pleasures of company and am a poor host... but I have sent Henrock out for some food. He will not be long. Visitors are a luxury we have almost forgotten and we have no provisions available. I trust your charming daughters slept well?' he added, turning to Joan and Julia.

The hand I shook seemed icy cold and although I only held it for a second I had the impression that there was something in the hand for my own palm seemed to touch something soft that tickled; but I forgot it a moment later for in turning to my daughters he had smiled and I saw that he too was afflicted by two gigantic and pointed eyeteeth! No wonder the poor man tried to keep his lips closed.

A second later he had closed his lips and I almost thought I must have been mistaken for now there was no hint of any abnormality as he stood, bending forward slightly, his tall figure clothed in a dark, close-fitting suit, a high black roll-collared pullover hiding some of the scragginess of his long and powerful neck. Even his shoes were black I noticed, slip-on boots with elastic sides, highly-polished.

'Well, yes,' replied Julia with some hesitancy. 'We were certainly tired and very grateful for the use of your bed but Joan had a nightmare and she doesn't seem to have recovered yet... are you all right Joan, you do look pale?'

'Yes, yes, I'm all right,' replied Joan dreamily. 'Well, actually, I'd like to lie down. Oh, sorry; we're just off aren't we? Mummy, could we go? I do feel a bit washed-out...'

'But my dear, I wouldn't think of it,' broke in our host. 'What would you think of me if I sent you away from this humble abode unwell? No, no, you must all be my guests until you are fit again for the journey.' 'No,' he insisted as I rose from my seat in protest. 'You will all consider yourselves my guests; and now,' he glanced towards the window where the first streaks of dawn were just beginning to show. 'Now I must ask you to excuse me. I too am tired after my journey and must rest; but Henrock will see that I am comfortable downstairs. Joan, you must return to bed and the rest of you please enjoy your day in our little village; I shall look forward to seeing you this evening...'

He turned abruptly and left us before we could say a word in reply.

Joan did look exhausted and needed little persuasion to return to bed. Her mother said she would stay with her so Julia and I returned our things upstairs and then thought we would go for a walk round the village.

As we left the house we met Henrock in the hall. 'The master tells me you are all staying for a while. I shall try to make you comfortable but I hope you will forgive the eccentricities of a lonely man and his servant of many years?'

I said we were very grateful for the kindness they were showing us and hoped we would not be too much trouble.

'Not at all,' replied Henrock. 'It will be pleasant to have guests again - but would you do one thing for us?'

'Yes, of course,' I replied and Julia nodded her consent. 'I'm very serious,' went on Henrock, almost stepping out of the shadows in his anxiety. 'It is a small thing but I want you to promise me something, nay I want you to swear by everything you hold dear, your wife and the girl upstairs. Swear you will do this one thing I ask.' Henrock's voice rose in fierce intensity.

We looked at each other. There was nothing we could do but agree. 'Of course, if it is within our power, we swear to do what you say,' I said, as lightly and evenly as I could. Henrock made us swear for my wife and Joan too and we wondered what on earth it could be that he was going to ask us to do; we were more than a little relieved when he said:

'It's very simple, but I'm serious. You must not talk to anyone in the village about us or this house, under any circumstances. You see they are a silly and superstitious people; they dislike my master and we have sworn never to have anything to do with anyone living there. You understand?' he concluded. 'You have solemnly sworn...'

'Yes, we understand,' I replied. 'We will not breathe a word.' With a bow of relief Henrock opened the door and we stepped out into the fresh morning air.

'Oh, we dine at night,' Henrock called to us from the doorway. 'There will be a good meal waiting for you then; conserve your appetite and you will enjoy the meal all the more, I promise you.'

Julia and I set off down the drive. We were both silent for a time, each occupied with our own thoughts - and fears. The weather was glorious after the stormy night and we soon arrived in sight of the drive gates when we both stopped dead in our tracks. Our car, which we had left parked on the outside of the locked gates, now stood within the gates!

I hurried forward but could find no explanation for the move. The drive gate was closed and the chain still secured. The lock still looked rusted and I would have said it had been unopened for months; the gate was quite immovable, and apparently the lock was rusted solid inside.

I turned my attention to the car. How on earth could it have been driven through anyway, since I had the keys? I unlocked and opened the car door. I tried the motor several times before it would turn over so I decided that some of the rain during the night's downpour must have found its way into the engine. There seemed little point in trying to get the car started just then in any case and I decided to leave it for the present, hoping it would dry out and start without difficulty later on.

As Julia and I climbed over the gate I saw to my amazement the clear tyre marks where I had left the car, now filled with water - but there were no traces of any marks through the gates and no signs of any marks where the car had been driven to its present position. If it had not been impossible I would have said the car had been lifted bodily over the gate and placed where it now stood!

With yet another problem to think about we set off up the hill away from the village in the direction of the hills, steaming in the morning sun.

For a time we walked side by side, silent and thoughtful. After a while I remembered that Julia had said she would tell me about Joan's nightmare. I asked her to tell me about it.

Julia looked at me for a moment. 'Well, it was very strange really. I was awakened by Joan's piercing scream but when I started up in alarm and asked what in heaven's name was the matter, she looked at me in surprise and asked what I meant. She hadn't realised that she had screamed but she said she felt sick and faint and thought she must have had a nightmare. She couldn't remember anything clearly but recalled the impression of an awful smell, like mouldy flesh, and said her neck felt sore. I thought she must have fallen asleep in an awkward position, and then she found her neck was bleeding. There seemed to be some pinpricks at the side of her neck and when we found an open safety-pin in the bed we decided that the combination of an accidental prick while she was asleep had triggered off her nightmare and scream. She was very quiet and listless but insisted that she was alright and told me to go back to sleep. Then you came in.'

We walked for hours, climbing most of the time. We stopped from time to time and at one point ate a bar of chocolate I had in my pocket. We could hardly believe it when we found that it was mid-afternoon, and we turned back. Far below us in the distance we could see the village we had left and we made our leisurely way back, weary but refreshed by the hours in the open air.

The sun had set and it was getting dark when we walked down the hill towards the big house and there we were met at the drive gate by my distressed wife who gasped out that she had been looking for us for hours but had no idea which direction we had taken. In frantic, broken sentences, she told us what had happened.

Soon after Joan had been put to bed she had fallen into a deep slumber. For a time my wife had sat by her side but she became frightened when Joan's breathing had quietened to such a degree that she had seemed to be hardly breathing at all. Uncertain what to do, among strangers in a strange house, she had run downstairs but had been unable to find anyone. Most of the doors she had tried had been locked; she could see no telephone and, thinking that Henrock must be somewhere in the grounds, she had gone out of the front door and made her way all round the house. She had discovered another drive that led to the rear of the house, a drive that disappeared among trees, high shrubs and bushes, but of Henrock there was no sign.

Frantic by this time, she had returned to the front of the house to find the door shut fast. She received no answer to her repeated knocking. She rushed down the front drive hoping to meet us returning and had tripped or stumbled in her hurry. She said she must have hit her head as she fell and knocked herself unconscious for the next thing she remembered was waking to find it was nearly dark. Her ankle was twisted and she was bleeding from the neck where she thought a briar must have caught her as she fell.

There were two neat punctures in her neck but little blood and I comforted her and told her we would find Joan and leave at once. As I held her to me she suddenly slumped into unconsciousness and I realised that the fall must have been a heavy one and she had hurt herself more than she had thought.

Between us Julia and I carried my wife up the drive and we were relieved to see a light in the room over the front door. At any rate someone was now at home. As we reached the door it was opened by Henrock who seemed genuinely alarmed and worried by the condition of my wife who was still unconscious.

With hardly a word of explanation we carried her upstairs and put her to bed in the room we had occupied; Henrock assisting and then standing watching us until she seemed as comfortable as we could make her.

'I must find a doctor at once,' I said to Henrock. 'Do you have a telephone? And how is Joan?'

Henrock motioned us to be quiet for the sake of my wife and led the way downstairs and into the room where we had earlier talked with his master. Once inside he guided us to the long seat by the window and took up a position himself by the piano.

The gist of the story he then related was that after he had assisted his master to retire and refresh himself, he had hurried out to fetch a doctor for Joan. When he returned with the doctor my wife was nowhere in sight but Joan was so ill that the doctor said she must go to hospital immediately and he would take her in his car, which he did.

Julia and I listened, wide-eyed and almost unbelieving, to all this but Henrock went on to say that the doctor was returning to talk to us about Joan and he expected him in fact at any moment, so he could look at my wife when he arrived. In the meantime,' concluded Henrock. 'My master hopes you will join him in the Long Room where a meal has been prepared for you.

How could we eat at such a time! But, as in a dream, Julia and I followed Henrock across the hall where he unlocked a door and lead us down a short passage and into a room where a table was laden with food. Sitting in a massive carved chair at the far end of the Long Room, away from the table, sat our host Damon Domain.

He rose from the chair in welcome but he did not move from the shadowy corner. 'My friends ... I hope you will forgive me but I have already dined. I am sure all your troubles will soon be over but in the meantime please eat a little of the food that Henrock has prepared and sample my vintage Romanian red wine, I think you will find it palatable...'

'You are most kind,' I managed to say, although food and drink were far from my thoughts at that moment. 'But I would like to see that my wife is comfortable first.' 'Of course,' the tall dark figure of the owner of this strange household agreed. 'Henrock, take our guest upstairs while I encourage his charming daughter to begin. You must be famished, my dear, after your long walk,' he added, turning to Julia.

I followed Henrock out of the room, back along the corridor and up the main staircase. At the door of the bedroom he halted for a moment and then threw open the door. The bedclothes were disarrayed but of my wife there was no sign! I turned aghast to Henrock for an explanation. He stood in the doorway, silent and sympathetic.

'I think it would be best not to mention this matter to your daughter,' he began. 'Not mention it...' I almost shouted. He looked pained at my tone. 'I'm afraid your wife was more seriously hurt than you thought... I was able to arrange for her immediate removal... you may see her soon,' he added, as I started towards him.

'She is quite safe,' he assured me. 'But she could not stay here without attention. You shall see her soon, I promise you. Now, please, the master is waiting.'

This *must* all be a dream I told myself as I started down the stairs ahead of Henrock; no, a nightmare. Surely I will wake up soon. I must.

Never shall I forget the scene that met my eyes when I walked into the Long Room which I had left only minutes before. Julia was slumped across the table, apparently unconscious, on her side, and over her bent Domain, his back towards me, his arms raised, drawing outwards the odd, dated, jacket-cape that he wore so that he looked for all the world like a great bat about to feed.

I darted forward and at my approach he turned. For a second I thought I saw again those awful fang-like teeth and a flash of some powerful and evil thing showed itself in the flashing eyes; but it all happened so quickly that immediately afterwards I thought I might have been mistaken; the look had gone and in its place the concerned and quiet man we knew as Damon Domain hurried towards me, his mouth almost closed but slightly smiling, spreading his hands in apology. 'My dear sir, a thousand apologies; there has been a little accident. Your daughter cut herself with a chipped wineglass and I was just doing what I could to assist. She seems to have fainted from shock but I am sure she will recover in a moment. Look - it really *id* a very little accident, the skin is just pricked on her neck - that's all.'

As I leaned over Julia her eyelids fluttered and I was about to ask her what had happened when she gave me one look so full of agonised hopelessness, the like of which I hope never to see again, and then lapsed back into unconsciousness.

She looked so terribly pale and lifeless that I was alarmed and taking her in my arms I laid her on the big settee by the wall where I felt she would be more comfortable. Having covered her with a thick woollen wrap that lay nearby, I turned to find that our host had hardly moved. He stood by the side of the table, drawn up to his full height; a commanding and forbidding figure. His eyes gleamed in the candle-light and his face seemed more bloated than when I had seen him previously. I turned towards the door where Henrock still stood, gazing in a hypnotic way at his master. I was in a quandary and for the first time I felt really frightened in this strange house with its stranger inmates.

'I must find a doctor,' I said at last. 'And I insist on seeing my wife. What on earth is going on?' I raised my voice but it had no effect upon my two hearers who remained motionless and silent.

Suddenly Damon Domain seemed to recover himself and looked at me afresh: 'Yes, yes, of course. We must make your daughter comfortable; but have no fear for she is a fine, healthy girl and will soon be quite fit again. Henrock: prepare a place for her to rest, near to her mother.'

Henrock turned and left the room but I was disturbed. What had Domain meant when he suggested that Julia be put somewhere near my wife? Something told me that all was far from well with my wife and my daughters and I ran after Henrock and caught him by the arm at the top of the stairs. I swung him round to face me. 'Now, look here. I've had about enough of all this. Take me to my wife at once.' He stared coldly at me. 'I think you should wait with the master. I will prepare somewhere for your daughter to rest and recover.'

So saying he turned to leave but in my anger, frustration and distress I lunged at him to swing him round again. Instead I knocked him off balance and before I could prevent it happening, he had crashed through the banister and fallen some twenty-five feet to the hall below!

Horror-stricken, I watched him fall and land with a sickening thud onto the stone floor. I knew that he must be terribly injured if not killed and I was about to rush down the stairs when, to my amazement, I saw him turn over on to his side, get up off the floor and walk across the hall and through the doorway, as though nothing untoward had happened!

Aghast I staggered back and, intending (I think) to make my way back to our host, I turned to find him at my shoulder. His face blazed with anger and fiendish power. Almost before I realised what was happening his powerful hands had seized me, my head was thrust sharply back and sideways and I caught a glimpse of those horrible fangs before I felt the sharp double-pain as he bit deep into the jugular vein, and I knew no more.

***

I awoke, i know not how long afterwards, to find myself lying on my back. It was dark and yet I found that I could see tolerably well. I seemed to be lying in some kind of box, and on earth! Good God! I was in a coffin of earth!

I started up but found myself weak beyond description. I felt drained of every drop of blood - as well I might be, I told myself.

In a way I had half-suspected the awful truth and looking back I realised that I should have known much sooner that we had stumbled into the retreat of a vampire!

What a fool I had been! It all seemed so obvious now that I couldn't think how I had not known almost as soon as we had arrived. I suppose (like most people) I unconsciously refused to believe that such things existed in the 1970s, but with my interest in the strange and the unusual I surely should have known.

The hostility of the villagers and their terror of the

dark; the niches over each doorway that must have been some kind of protective amulet; even the garlic which no vampire can face. The fearsome fangs of Henrock and of his master who arrived at night in that terrible storm. The way their eyebrows met over the nose and of course it was hair in the palm that I had felt when I had shaken hands. My skin shivered at the thought. The way both of them had always positioned themselves so that they did not reveal the tell-tale fact that they cast no shadows. The absence of any mirror in the house; and no cross of any kind; why even their shoes had no laces! *They* had never partaken of any food or drink in our presence. Superhuman strength that could lift a car over a gate. A heavy fall had not harmed Henrock for he was invincible except against garlic, a cross or a stake through the heart!

While all this was passing through my mind I lay, exhausted, gazing up at the ceiling; but gradually I felt a little stronger and at length I pulled myself up and looked around me. Even as I had dreaded yet knew in my heart, there were other boxes similar to that wherein I lay. Five more were spread about the room or dungeon, I knew not what it was.

A little longer and I felt able to rise and lift my weary limbs. I forced myself to climb out of the box and leave the sickening damp and earthy bed.

Slowly I crawled over to the nearest box. There lay my dear wife, pale and hardly breathing with the telltale trickle of blood from the two pricks in her white neck. I tried to wake her, uncontrollable tears running down my cheeks, but she seemed to be in a deep coma of some kind. I stepped across the room and found my dear daughters in a similar condition. They looked so pale but so beautiful. I wept unashamedly, found myself slipping to the floor, and must have lost consciousness.

I awakened Again in darkness. This was no dream! I was still in this accursed room with the unconscious bodies of my dear family. I pulled myself upright and tried to think what I could do. There might not be much time. In fact there was no time to help any of us. We were already doomed but if only I could stop this nest of vampires.

I pumped my brain to recollect what I could of vampires and vampirism. They could not face a cross, I knew that. But how could that help me now. At least, perhaps, I could protect my family from further assaults if only I could fashion some crosses. How, oh heavens, how?

I forced myself to reach the other two occupied boxes or coffins. They were empty but the impressions in them left no doubt in my mind that they were the resting-places of Henrock and his master. Soon, I guessed, it would be dawn and then they would come to take their rest - perhaps they would even come for a final feed - before remaining imprisoned in their boxes during the hours of daylight. I had no time to lose.

How could I manufacture three crosses, even four. Frantically I looked around me. There were no windows and, apart from the boxes, nothing but a few odds and ends in the room. Broken furniture, newspapers, some petrol cans, an old mattress - nothing that I could see would help me, and yet...

I seized a broken chair and a leg came off in my hand. I looked again at the unoccupied boxes. Could I perhaps conjure up some crosses from the wood of the boxes? It seemed worth a try.

Using the chair leg as a hammer I broke off the ends of one box, one piece of wood after the other; then the other end. By now I felt weak with fatigue but I forced myself to attack the other unoccupied box in the same way. This done I took two narrow pieces of wood and placing one across the other in the form of a cross, I placed it gently over the dear pale face of my sleeping wife. Then I did the same for my daughters. Taking two of the larger pieces of wood from the side of one box I succeeded in forming a huge cross which I balanced against the box I had laid in so that it faced the door and might dissuade whoever or whatever came through the door.

Really exhausted now I slumped to the floor in an agony of despair. What could I do to save my family. Oh God! Must I fashion stakes and pierce their lovely bodies? And what could I do to stop these fiends for ever?

Suddenly I remembered fire. Vampires cannot withstand fire! Could I set fire to this cursed place and rid the world of these wretched creatures?

I struggled to my feet again and made my way across the room to where the rubbish lay. There was paper and it was dry. The mattress, too, might burn. I looked carefully around me. The door was wooden and the posts, which looked very old and dry should burn if only I could get them well alight. Then I saw the petrol cans. I pulled one out. It was empty. Then another; that was empty too. A third had some petrol in it! A fourth was full! And a fifth!

I hesitated for only a moment. I knew what I had to do. I took more pieces of wood from the sides of the broken boxes; split the wood by bending it against itself with the help of the chair leg, and so I fashioned three stakes.

I tore the mattress apart, crumpled the paper against the door and doorposts, spread the contents of the mattress over and around the paper, piled the rest of the wood from the broken boxes and the remains of the chair and the bits and pieces of furniture in a conical shape against the door. I poured all the petrol I could find over it. I found my pocket lighter and was about to set light to the paper when I stopped. The whole house was as quiet as death. To ensure the destruction of Henrock and his master I must at least be sure that they were in the house. Dare I wait until I could be sure that they were both at home?

I sat back on the floor and rested. Yes, I decided I would try to delay setting light to the rubbish and, hopefully, to the house, until I heard some sound that suggested that 'they' were within the walls of Domdaniel. 'Domdaniel', I thought, how aptly named, 'an infernal dwelling.'

Author's Note. The above account, in a minute hand, was written in a pocket notebook which was discovered in a remote Scottish village in an empty petrol can in the cellar of an isolated house which had been completely destroyed by fire. Also in the cellar the remains were found of three female bodies in earth-filled coffins and the remains of a man lay on the floor, on his back with legs straight together and arms outstretched at right angles, in the form of a cross. Outside what had been the door of the cellar police reported finding two huge piles of thick dust that stank abominably. When disturbed the dust disintegrated and disappeared.

TO CLAIM HIS OWN

by Crispin Derby

[CRISPIN DERBY (BORN 1948) is a journalist and is currently deputy editor of a leading specialist weekly magazine. He has contributed to a wide range of journals. He is a keen sportsman, gardener and lover of wild and domestic creatures - particularly when cooked. He tends to disparage the occult in general and confesses only to an insatiable craving for vampire literature, films and facts. He is a blood donor.]

'Brass candlesticks ... human heads ... and ... Willi seemed to fall backwards, downwards ... down and down ...'

It was three o'clock in the morning in East Berlin. A tall dark figure passed speedily across the frost-gripped park towards Karl Marx Allee. Prewar tenements rose grimly on the right while, across the broad highway, stood the modern concrete tributes to communist architecture.

Quicker and yet quicker strode his feet until they seemed to barely touch the ground. He was quite alone in the street.

As he approached the garish lights of the luxurious Berolina Hotel, he crossed the road holding aloft an arm as if in protest against the painfully bright illuminations.

He crossed rapidly, though picking carefully through the tramlines in the centre. As he reached the other side a grey uniformed policeman, with pistol at his side, casually stepped out of an alleyway. The man walked past him head down and with hat pushed firmly over his brow, hiding his pallid face.

The policeman watched him go but felt a sudden chill cut through him for which he could not account. But then, the man was heading directly towards the forbidden Berlin Wall.

'I should have stopped him,' he thought. Then he radioed the nearest command post on the edge of the barbed-wired noman's-land approaching the Wall.

The man walked on, his footsteps silent on the frost-whitened pavements. Then he ran out of street lights and the night grew black as he came into sight of the bricked-up tenements that marked the two-hundred-yard zone on the east side of the Wall.

There were distant spotlights, barbed wire and soldiers' huts littered about. Two conscript guards were idly chattering while taking sly drags at an inferior cigarette. The man saw the clouds of smoke and hot breath puffing out of their chilled bodies and strode out of the shadows towards them.

As he came within a hundred yards of them the radio message came through to give the alert. In a flash the cigarette was trampled on and the machine guns were cocked.

He instinctively sought the shadows but could clearly be seen. The guards moved forward. So did he. The young guards did their best to look menacing but he seemed oblivious. With head down his tall slender figure moved inexorably forwards. They turned towards each other feeling horribly lonely.

'He's a bold one, huh!' said one.

'We're for it if we don't challenge,' replied his friend nervously fingering the gun. and praying that his authority wouldn't be tested.

As the man came within twenty yards the taller guard barked out as fiercely as he could.

'Achtung, Achtung.'

But the words stuck in his throat. A cloud of dense fog appeared from nowhere bringing foul vapours, filling their lungs with choking smog. They clutched at the air and then at their throats as they fell staggering wildly about. In minutes the fog had cleared, or so it seemed. But as the guards hastened to contact their colleagues at the Wall itself the fog reappeared cloaking the concrete ramparts and disappearing slowly, but inevitably westwards.

***

Herr Kurt Muller, a middle grade official on the Mayor of Berlin's staff, was stumbling out of a nightclub in the city's vice quarter with his favourite hostess beside him. He had passed through the incapability of drunkenness and was coming back to stark reality. He was determined to finish the evening improperly, but was beginning to be seized with guilt lest his wife should find out. As he pushed his hand at the glass exit door a tall dark man stood outside as though poised to enter.

'They're closing, they're closing,' slurred Kurt pushing outwards.

The man stretched himself to full height in response and for the first time that night in Berlin his face was fully visible. The chalky pallor was perceived even by the fuddled bureaucrat. Only a tint of high rose at the crest of his cheekbones and on his thin drawn lips gave any sign of life. A high forehead led only to a black Homburg under which peeped sleek black hair. But the eyes. Kurt had never seen such eyes. Huge whites with bulging red veins stared into his face. The blue irises burned into his soul completely paralysing him. Kurt stumbled soberly aside.

The man raced downstairs. He stepped as surely into the darkness as if he were a regular. When he reached the cabaret floor it was quite empty, save for a swarthy, stocky German in evening dress. He rose in agitation.

'Dr Kocsis. So you have come!'

The tall man inclined his head with less than a nod, but enough to signify assent.

'Where is my property, Glick?' The words came out precisely, without character or intonation.

'It is on its way Doctor. It will be here within the hour.' Glick kept his back firmly to the wall.

'The hour, Glick? Do you realise it is five o'clock now?'

'It was delayed at the border. There are rigorous searches these days, you must appreciate.'

'I was not delayed at the border. Ha. I shall not be delayed at any mere mortal barriers, nor shall my property. I spared no expense. You realise what will happen to you if you fail me?'

Glick looked down and silently prayed.

Suddenly a noise broke the hypnotic silence and a man, blond and thirtyish entered wearing jeans and a jerkin.

'It is ready sir. It is in the cellar. Have you the money?'

'Here.' Glick thrust forward a package. He turned back to the Doctor smiling with relief - but he was already speeding towards the cellar.

'Wunderbar, wunderbar,' muttered the policeman, adjusting his tie in the club's cracked dressing-room mirror. He grinned at himself foolishly. He gently fingered the remains of an old scar received during the war from an SS man's rifle butt. Then, remembering his position he checked his equipment, especially the pistol - after all he could be the subject of a trick. But no, surely this little Heidi wouldn't trick him the second time round. He looked down at her on the tousled couch. As she said, they were irresistibly attracted to each other. Just a week ago she had spirited him from his lonely, boring beat and tempted him into the best lovemaking he could remember. How could he refuse a second chance when she ran after him tonight? He bent down to kiss her forehead. She was asleep -having made sure of keeping him from his beat for an hour.

As he stepped out of the club's back door to resume his work a dingy barge slipped away from the nearby quayside. He strolled on whistling tunelessly until a thick mist sprang up and douched his spirit.

Inside the barge a huge bald German stood resolutely at the wheel peering ahead. He said nothing to the man beside him who was now anxiously studying maps with a short, muscular, blue-chinned individual over an oil-lit table.

'Stop worrying,' said blue-chin in thick middle-European accents. 'We leave you at Amsterdam so there is nothing to fear. We have a warehouse ready. You are paid enough so just shut up and concentrate on your part of the job.'

'But what is in those boxes, Vasaly?'

The powerful Vasaly stood up slowly, turned to stare at his questionner and then turned away to join his helmsman. They conversed briefly in sign language and then Vasaly returned.

'I'm going to get some sleep now, Willi. Just make sure that you don't move or my friend, Ferenc, will crush you into tiny pieces.'

As if he had heard, the bald giant wheeled round and with vacant expression motioned with his hands as if wringing out a dish-cloth.

Willi shuddered and studied his feet for a long five minutes. How damp this barge was, how cold and how terrifying. At any time the river police could stop them and they'd be sure to find the boxes. And what was in them? Guns, probably. Or drugs. If he only hadn't gambled so much he would never have got into this trouble. That *schweinhund* Glick and his sleazy club. And that vixen Heidi. It almost seemed as if they had planned to trap him. He wouldn't have let them use his barge like this if it wasn't the only way out of his troubles. And what was his wife supposed to think of it all? Willi coughed despairingly and slipped a piece of dusty *wurst* out of his pocket to chew on.

As Willi whimpered into dreamland it seemed ever colder. But as he dreamed a sudden warm draught appeared to beat down upon his face. This was followed by the slightest sting which half-roused him and then left him sleeping deeper than ever.

The smell of frying sausage and tomato awoke Willi the next damp morning. He dimly perceived Vasaly holding a black pan over a spirit stove of ancient make and design. Still at the helm was the statuesque Fernec peering endlessly ahead as if he could just make out the North Pole in the far distance.

'You've slept well Willi, come and have a sausage,' said Vasaly.

Willi nodded. 'I will. That sleep did me good though the draughts in this tub have given me a hell of a stiff neck.'

Vasaly's improved humour and the warm breakfast combined to cheer Willi up.

'Doesn't Ferenc eat breakfast? He's stood there for two days now. He doesn't even go to the lavatory?' Willi ventured grinning.

Ferenc turned slowly from the wheel and, zombie-like, fixed Willi with a long cold stare. Willi shivered and resumed his silent agitation.

The barge chugged on, almost permanently shrouded in murky damp mist that got right down into Willi's stomach. 'Come on Amsterdam,' he kept saying to himself.

That night he dreamed again. This time it seemed that he was lying on a marble slab, naked. The ceiling and walls around him were covered with blood-red baize. Brass candlesticks burned on velvet covered tables scattered about the room. And all the time black, undistinguishable figures with human heads seemed to fall down upon him from the ceiling.

The next night he dreamed the same dream with trivial deviations. And then again - so vivid that he began to spend his days pondering it and hardly noticing the routine of Vasaly's simple cooking and Ferenc's silent steering. All he noticed was a weakening, lack-lustre feeling. An overwhelming apathy that almost pleased him by quenching his former nervousness. It was the perfect sedative. He remembered verses from Tennyson's *Lotus-Eaters* that summed up his feelings.

And deep asleep he seem'd, yet all awake,

And music in his ears his beating heart did make.

His only discomfort was this damned pain in his neck. 'Curse this draughty hulk,' he muttered. Vasaly broke through Willi's reverie.

'We'll be in Amsterdam tomorrow night. Better get some sleep now. There'll be plenty of work in the morning.'

Willi drifted off without a word. Again the dream came to him, but this time clearer, more certain. He was not afraid, simply passive and helpless. The figures still fell down on him. One after another. Over and over again. Willi just lay, seeming to fall backwards, downwards as though he were dropping slowly down a bottomless mine shaft. Suddenly there was a great booming noise from a ship's hooter. He awoke with a start and then an anguished howl as he felt a piercing needle of pain in his neck. A dark shape scurried off and Willi thrust his hand up to his aching neck. He held it there to soothe and then reached for his handkerchief. As he pulled it away from his neck he saw it was stained with blood.

His heart thundered like a pneumatic hammer. He gasped with terror. What on earth had happened?

'Vasaly, Ferenc,' he cried. Vasaly entered the cabin.

'Quiet you fool, we are going through town. Do you want to spoil the whole plan? Look you've scratched yourself in your sleep. Here is some water. Clean it up.'

Willi feebly dabbed at his bruised neck with the ice-cold water. He felt miserable, lonely and cold again. Yet at the same time his forehead was feverishly warm.'

'Vasaly', he cried. 'Have you a mirror? I want to look at the damage to my neck.'

Again Ferenc made one of his chilling turns from the wheel and stared at Willi. As he turned back to his horizon-gazing he let out a long rasping series of chuckles. A laugh that was singularly uncontagious. Willi dropped the subject. In any case his beard covered the mark, he comforted himself.

As the day wore on Willi continued drowsing weakly and mopping his hot brow. He was now convinced that he had influenza and that it was caused by worry and the accursed damp. He couldn't understand why his own staff hadn't complained.

He knew the outskirts of Amsterdam had at least been reached. Vasaly was almost permanently out of the barge making mysterious preparations but Willi had so little strength and felt so apathetic that he couldn't rouse the enthusiasm to ask what was going on.

For days, it seemed weeks, he had sat or laid in the damp cabin in this smelly barge. All he had seen were shrouds of mist, the occasional glimpse of a frosted bulb field and the odd giant windmill. He had heard the sinister creakings of the sails and plenty of foghorns and riverside shouts and clamour. He had heard lock gates opening and closing, opening and closing, and closing and opening. Now he heard the clanging of ships' bells, more foghorns and the noisier hammering of the dockyard. He was in Amsterdam and would soon be disembarking. His reverie was interrupted as Vasaly returned.

'Wake up Willi. I have to go ashore again. I want you to do something for me tonight. You might appreciate it and it would satisfy your curiosity.'

'What is it Vasaly? When will I go home? I think I have the 'flu. It is the damp here, you know.'

'Stop your rambling, fool. Come you must guard the boxes for me. Ferenc will be the first line of resistance here, but you must stay in the hold. Mind you don't tamper with them. You will be making the biggest mistake of your life if you do.' Willi was past caring and simply tottered off the couch and followed Vasaly to the door. He turned to look at Ferenc, who he could sense was staring after him. The big man was, and grinned like a dervish. Willi did not notice Vasaly lock the door as he left. He was propped up in a chair alone with the oblong boxes. Still gripped by apathy he slumbered off again.

But he awoke with a sharp jolt. One of the boxes right in front of him was wide open. Wild-eyed he whimpered low. 'My God they'll crucify me.'

He staggered forward to look inside, half believing it was another dream. The box was lined with moist sedge peat. The brown crumbly interior was musty and quite empty.

In the gloom he sensed a figure. In the corner. Just over his right shoulder. Willi turned slowly, forcing himself, willing himself to look, yet terribly afraid.

It was a slender giant, well over six feet tall with jet black hair, fierce piercing eyes and the whitest face he had ever seen.

He noticed the high cheekbones which set deep

shadows in the jowls and the uncanny effect of the rose-red lips. He was dressed in white tie and tails, the whole surmounted by a floor-length cape of dense black velvet. The cape was fixed with a brooch of some strange metal which clasped a giant ruby that spectacularly reflected the small degree of light.

He appeared to be looking way over the top of Willi's head - an expression of noble suffering on his pale face. Willi could see the arms crossed like a saint under the cloak. Willi shuddered and felt icy cold. He wanted to flee but was glued to the spot. He opened his mouth but no words came. He wanted to look but couldn't.

The man lowered his eyes to gaze on trembling Willi. They stared at each other for some moments.

'Come Willi,' said a deep, rich voice so low that it might have sprung from the earth's own vaults.

Willi obediently moved forward, hardly conscious of his physical frailty. He dragged his feet across the dimlit room and stood by the man. The smell in the hold was overpowering but Willi was determined not to faint.

'You see my brooch, Willi?' Willi nodded. 'Examine it carefully.' Willi turned his head to one side and stared closely at the twinkling ruby. It seemed to send shafts of silver bright light deep into his brain. He watched mesmerised and began to recall his dream. And now there was the hot breath on his face, on his cheek, on his neck. And then the sharp prick, a sting as if from a giant hornet. A sensation as though two diamond-tipped hypodermics were plunging into him, deeper and deeper and then the long, hot feeling of powerful suction as if the life-blood were being drawn from his veins.

***

Sir Bernard Mathews was grey-faced and drawn as he shuffled into the restaurant car of the Cambridge train at Harwich, East Anglia's main passenger seaport. His sheepskin jacket was drawn tightly around his stocky frame; his grey goatee beard was held low and his brown cossack hat was firmly clamped over his thick white thatch. The sharp east wind blew off the North Sea as it does for eight months of the year in those parts. But Sir Bernard was unconcerned. Certainly he felt uncomfortable. But this derived more from the severely troubled spirit evidenced in his deeply furrowed brow and his dark shadowed, red-rimmed eyes.

He was on his way to his old friend Charles Devereux at one of the oldest Cambridge colleges. There he knew he would receive an understanding and, at first, unquestioning audience. Meanwhile he barely noticed the quiet courtesies of bright-red-uniformed restaurant car attendants who brought him his much needed pot of tea and hot, buttered teacake. He looked out on the bleak Fenland countryside as the train sped towards Cambridge, which, to Sir Bernard, spelled sanity.

Without any signs of approaching a city, the train pulled into Cambridge station and Sir Bernard hastily organised porters to place his luggage with a cab driver who took him to the college where Charles Devereux was Senior Fellow.

Charles Devereux felt slightly irritated as he put away the last of the apple pie and the very last of the whipped cream accompaniment. Why on earth was Bernard so damned urgent all of a sudden? They had known each other for nearly forty years and he couldn't remember a time that Bernard had *demanded* to see him and insisted on board and lodging until further notice. It wasn't like him. It was discourteous. But Charles Devereux was nevertheless glad to see him.

As he passed from the panelled hall into the lobby that led to the senior common room, Sir Bernard sprang at him and gripped his arm like the *Ancient Mariner*.

'Charles. Thank God you're here.'

'How lovely to see you Bernard. But what on earth is all this cloak and dagger stuff? You've quite put me out, though of course it is very good to see you. Especially if I can be of some service.'

'I am so worried Charles, I just don't know where to begin.'

'Well let me help by dragging you into the common room to join us. I'd like to present a bottle of Port to celebrate your appearance.'

'No, Charles, I really couldn't. Not in this state. Can't we talk privately?'

'I am firmly resolved Bernard. You must relax after your long journey. Unwind a little. You'll be able to explain more coherently I am sure. Besides - your appearance will do me a power of good in the election for the new master of the college next month.'

The fire blazed in the senior common room and the flames reflected brightly from the light, highly polished oak panelling and the multi-faceted port glasses which were intermittently replenished from the bottle - passed clockwise of course.

Sir Bernard did indeed begin to unwind and settled himself in next to Charles who delighted in the introductions between his fellow dons and his distinguished guest.

It was near eleven o'clock before they were left alone with twin glowing faces, slightly fuddled, and Sir Bernard, certainly, feeling jollier than for many days.

Charles lingered over writing the inscription in the famous college book that now recorded the fact that on this night Charles Devereux, Senior Fellow of this college, presented a bottle in honour of his distinguished guest, Sir Bernard Mathews, the most famous and honoured pathologist crime has ever known.

'Well, what brings you here, Bernard, and in such unaccustomed haste, and, dare I say, agitation?'

Sir Bernard sat silent for a few moments and stared into the pile of the ancient carpet, gathering his thoughts. He began haltingly.

'I have seen the most chilling sight that any criminal pathologist can have seen for years.'

'Come, come,' responded Charles. 'You are the last person to flinch at any horror inflicted by human beings. What on earth was it?'

'What on earth? Inflicted by human beings? That's just it. That's just it. You'll think me mad when I explain.'

'I shall definitely go mad with curiosity if you don't get on and tell me Bernard.'

'Well, I was in Amsterdam attending the European branch conference. Because Johaan lives there I had arranged to stay with him for the week which was very nice although I was at the conference most of the time and he was working. Nevertheless.'

'Get on Bernard.'

'I'm sorry. On the last day of the conference I had just sat down when an attendant raced in to call me to the telephone. Johaan wanted to speak to me urgently. So, I went out to the telephone wondering what it could be. If I had known in advance I think I would have turned straight for home. The implications of this thing are just too dreadful to contemplate.' 'For heaven's sake, Bernard, come to the point,' Charles snapped.

'The point is this,' Bernard said taking a grip on himself. 'Johaan insisted I go straightaway to a mortuary in the dockland and there was the body of a German which had been recovered from a little-used canal in Amsterdam itself.'

'He was drowned?'

'He was certainly full of water. He must have been there for three or four days. But do you know? Nay, would you believe there was barely a drop of blood in him?'

Sir Bernard stopped Charles's gasps. 'That's not all.' He had fully recovered his composure. 'Johaan then pointed out to me two clear marks in the neck where *something*, I'm being careful with my words, was clearly used to draw the blood from the man. In fact on examination it was proved that the man had been bled to death - literally bled white before being dumped in the canal. Now, let me go on Charles, Johaan - he is of course my opposite number in Holland as you know - just stayed silent while I made the examination. After I had made my own full examination at his request he showed me the certificate of death wherein he made no mention of the real questions. For reasons of political necessity he hushed it up and the poor German's family will fortunately never know his fate.

'Johaan's first question was am I mad? He wanted desperately to know if I was thinking what he was thinking. I was. And hard though we tried to think of an alternative we could not.

'The Dutch government has two top men working on the criminal aspects. This killer must be traced before anything worse happens. He has a week's start on them almost.'

'Have they got anywhere?'

'They have made considerable progress. They know that a mysterious barge somehow reached Amsterdam from Germany without apparently going through any Customs' checks and without registering at the Dock. It managed to unload a cargo of some half dozen oblong heavy boxes with unknown contents.

'A wellknown Dutch transvestite later was discovered to have put pressure on certain shady shipowners with a view to taking this cargo on a voyage of unknown destination but a journey of "about a hundred miles".'

'How many days is the cargo missing?'

'Only two, but we do not know where it is going or if it has left.'

'What do you think, Charles? You know about such things. That is why I have come to you. Is it a vampire?'

Charles, almost sobered by now, turned to face the dying fire. He looked extremely tired and his brow was now as deeply furrowed as Sir Bernard's.

'I am afraid it is, and I fear that I know what he is after.'

***

The little tugboat chugged up to and tied alongside the Liberian registered ship *Parkdirecteur* as it lay at anchor in the little estuary off the Essex coast. In the distance twinkled the lights of the army town of Colchester. Half an hour saw six boxes unloaded and the tug pulled away with its new cargo and two accompanists ... A swarthy Hungarian and tall, broad-shouldered, bald mute.

The cockney tugboatman and his son, helping him, said nothing to the men. They were experienced enough to know better than to ask questions. It was still dark as they made towards the tiny fishing port of Brightlingsea - once the scene of a cruel polio epidemic - and now the witness of the arrival of something more horrific, more contagious, and more utterly evil than anything in the history of Great Britain.

The tug didn't stop there. The tide was high and it was able to navigate the difficult channels of the little creek that led two miles inland to the historic village of St Osyth, along a path followed centuries before by Danish invaders who carried off the nuns from the old priory.

The boat tied up. The owner and his son helped Vasaly and Ferenc to unload the boxes into a waiting lorry. Ferenc and Vasaly climbed in and drove off leaving full payment.

'Well, mate. There's a grand easily earned. Better than mucking about with the Pakis. I wonder where they're being taken?'

'Soon find out Dad. Most of them get caught these days. Even we can't dodge Customs and coastguards every time.'

'Well, they won't catch those buggers. Too bloody clever.'

As Ferenc and Vasaly pressed on through the wintry dawn the countryside changed subtly from seaside bare to the lusher pastures of North Essex farmland. Towards the wheatfields of North East Essex and into the bare and desolate Fens. It was nearing eight o'clock on a damp Shrove Tuesday morning when they turned off the main road onto a minor road. Soon after crossing the rivers - banked up above the surrounding land - they turned down a narrow gravel track which led to a country house called Grunty Abbey isolated in some uncultivated black Fenland.

The bare furnishings of this recently vacated small monastery greeted the men. Only Vasaly showed signs of tiredness and looked quite hunchbacked with his weary stoop. Ferenc and Vasaly passed silently from room to room and grunted mutually before returning to the lorry.

Taking pickaxe handles from the cab they stomped back to the abbey and then went through the entire building smashing and defacing every last relic of religious significance in the building. When the exhausting toil was completed Vasaly looked at Ferenc and nodded. He then lay down on the stone floor and slept.

Ferenc stared, grinning and then walked to the window to gaze endlessly across the perfectly flat Fenland where the wind howled, it seemed, perpetually.

It was almost as if Ferenc could see right across the twenty miles of flat agricultural land to Cambridge itself, where lights betrayed the presence of Sir Bernard and Charles locked in dialogue in Charles's rooms.

No longer were there the signs of agitation that marked their first discussion of the vampire's advent. Now they were calm, thoughtful, like generals mapping out a campaign which they were determined to succeed in. Vivaldi's *Four Seasons* played softly in the background as Charles poured another glass of claret each.

'This news from Johaan is remarkable, Bernard. At least the monster has come where someone is ready for him.'

Bernard still toyed with the telegram he had just received from Amsterdam. He read it again to make sure all the details were firmly embedded in his mind.

Amsterdam Sunday stop cargo traced to ship called Park-directur left Rotterdam Friday with illegal immigrants bound for England stop UK Government informed stop over to Special Branch stop they will contact you stop strictest secrecy naturally stop Johaan

'The extraordinary thing is, Charles, nobody thinks the idea is mad.'

'Wait till we meet Special Branch. That is if I am allowed to.'

'You're involved Charles. There is no question of that.'

Just as Vivaldi's *Winter* drew to a close the door was

rapped on sharply three times.

'Talk of the devil.' laughed Charles.

The opened door revealed a young man in his late twenties. A single-breasted navy blue raincoat covered him to his knees where black serge trousers led to black brogues. Charles looked up to the young pale face with the thick black hair cut short and the hawkish nose.

'Special branch,' said the young man. 'I'm Roger Bentall.' 'Are you gentlemen Charles Devereux and Sir Bernard Mathews?'

Charles nodded open-mouthed. He gestured Bentall to sit down and he shut the door after him. He turned back into the room and muttered ironically 'in strictest secrecy'.

Introductions completed, they briefed Bentall. Having arrived almost completely ignorant he fell in keenly with their plans. They were soon on first name terms with only one bottle emptied.

'Er, Roger is there just you on this project?' queried Charles.

'Yes, though I may request support.'

'Mmmm. Perhaps it's just as well.' He glanced at Bernard who looked more worried every minute.

'Before you go, Roger, you must tell us which hotel you are at. We may need to contact you,' said Charles.

'Hotel, Charles? I'm to stay here. Even if it means sleeping on the floor. I have my instructions, I'm sorry.'

'Good God. Does that mean you're shadowing us?' Sir Bernard spluttered.

'No sir. But if this is as urgent as I'm told we'll just have to live in each others' pockets until this case is solved. Or at least until the danger is past.'

'This danger will never be past, Roger,' Charles gravely intoned fixing his eyes on those of the young detective.

As Roger lay uncomfortably on the green velvet chaise-longue that night a soft fall of several inches of snow turned that part of Cambridgeshire into a vast flat white desert.

Vasaly shivering in the newly-occupied abbey turned and woke to find his giant master towering over him menacingly, with lips drawn back over the piano keyboard teeth.

'Doctor,' gasped Vasaly, writhing backwards in fear.

'Tremble not, my son. You know your duty. Go forth and find my children.'

'Yes, master.'

'Do not fail me Vasaly. Or...' Doctor Kocsis lifted his staring eyes. They were more bloodshot than ever. He peered high into the darkness and was rewarded with a wolf-like howl from somewhere out in the Fen. His face relaxed and he left the room.

It was almost dawn. At first light Vasaly set off. He soon reached the mediaeval buildings surrounding the castle-like cathedral built on a mound of clay rising eighty feet out of the Fens. He spent the morning studying the town and learning the relationships of buildings and streets and then found a greasy cafe for a fry-up lunch. He greedily eyed the waitress but got no reaction.

After lunch he went to a dingy pub near the waterside where he took pains to get into conversation with the landlord and a few customers - farm labourers and the like. Some US servicemen from a nearby base mingled with the locals and Vasaly managed to include himself in their chatter. He quickly learned that they were a magnet for local girls and promised to return that evening to join the fun.

As night fell Vasaly returned to the pub. He tucked into a rump steak and a huge pile of chips before beginning to drink. His friends arrived as promised and he carried on drinking. Later the servicemen arrived and then the much vaunted girls. Vasaly was soon introduced to the USAF camp followers. A wide age range with an appeal based on fading youth and exposure of flesh. There was little pretence at beauty but much reliance on acreage of thigh and bosom.

Vasaly was quite drunk by the time he found himself clinging to Thelma's waist. The plain, well-built girl was attracted to his strange 'mittel european' ways. In the thick roaring crowd it was no embarrassment to cling tighter and then to kiss, hotly and passionately.

The pub began to sway as the now drunken throng sang raucous songs that Vasaly joined in as best he could. Arms were linked, beer was slopped and more and more embraces were exchanged.

In the throng Vasaly was able to cling closer to Thelma. The free manner in which she pressed bosom and hips into him was ample proof to Vasaly that he had found a friend.

The bell clanged closing time shortly before the grand cathedral clock boomed out eleven o'clock. Vasaly employed drinking-up time in swapping kisses and making arrangements. Thelma told him the village where she lived - divorced, childless and alone.

As they tumbled out of the pub a car drew up alongside. 'My car,' said Vasaly with chivalry. 'You must have a few bob, then,' giggled Thelma.

They climbed in the back to resume their cuddles. Ferenc released the clutch and they sped off out of town across the humped river bridge and out among the desolate Fen highways.

They arrived at Thelma's tiny cottage and clambered out of the car. Vasaly quickly opened the door and pushed her inside. He held her, moved closer, and Thelma responded greedily.

At four o'clock in the morning Vasaly awoke. As he regained his wits he became aware of a scratching at the window. A tap-tapping that made him all too conscious of his role in life.

He dressed, left Thelma sleeping and slipped quietly out through the front door. As he stepped trembling towards the car an arm like a steel girder grabbed him from behind, jerking his tousled head backwards.

Vasaly turned his eyes upwards in fear and trepidation. The fearsome face of Dr Kocsis glowered at him. His head was pushed sideways, his collar ripped from his shirt. Vasaly shrank from him and tried to struggle away but it was useless. The doctor had an unbreakable grip. Vasaly tried to scream as he saw the Doctor's head slowly easing down towards his neck. He felt the breath on his face and then the Doctor moved his mouth slightly upward to Vasaly's ear. And he whispered menacingly, 'Remember who you serve.'

The grip was released and Vasaly raced to the car followed more sedately by the Doctor. As Vasaly cooled down he determined to do his duty. That devil. 'Hah,' he spat angrily.

* * *

Peter Devereux, Charles's brother, was carefully opening his post on a bright winter's morning in his old timbered office when he was struck by a rather unusual missive. He couldn't quite place what was odd about it; it simply felt rather strange. It was one of those funny things that he and his brother Charles often spent long evenings mulling over and arguing about.

He opened and quickly read the neat thick black writing. He called out to his young daughter.

'Marie, quick, come and look at this.

The letter read:

To Peter Devereux, Editor, The Fen Gazette.

Dear Mr Devereux,

I am newly arrived in your country from Romania and would welcome the aquaintance of one so knowledgeable on local lore and customs. Perhaps you would be kind enough to dine with me one evening at my humble home. You may bring a guest.

Your grateful friend.

Dr Kocsis.

Peter excitedly held the letter while Marie peered over his shoulder.

'Do you know him, Dad?'

'I should say so. He's been persecuted by the Communists ever since they took over his country. He is one of the old-time aristocracy, accustomed to ruling the peasants with an iron hand. They've tried to discredit him in all sorts of outlandish ways and they've tried physical attacks. But he's a remarkable old boy and has resisted everything.'

'But how did he get here then?'

'Escaped, I suppose. Probably things got too hot even for him.'

'Does Uncle Charles know him?'

'Ha. You know Charles. Chats all right about myths and fantasy but pin him down to politics or anything real and he clams up. He's always hinted at knowing something but won't say. Treats me like a judge who's going to ask him to produce evidence.'

'Will you tell him then, Dad?'

'No. No, I don't think I will. I shall accept the invitation and return it sometime, making sure that Charles comes too. I shall go certainly, and you will come with me I hope.'

'I really shan't understand a word he says.'

'I will translate for you, Marie.'

On the night of their dinner, Peter and Marie took extra care with their appearance for this special occasion. Peter, a longtime fan of any and everyone who defied Communists, and Marie his beautiful sixteen-year-old daughter just looking forward to a rare sophisticated evening out.

Peter brushed a few silver hairs from his black velvet evening suit and straightened the big matching bow. He eventually slipped off the cummerbund thinking it 'a bit much', as he would say.

Marie adjusted the neckline of the post office red gown for the twentieth time. She decided the dress probably didn't go well with long ash blond hair and blue eyes but it was too late now. While she was about it she decided that she was perhaps just a little plump.

They set off in their big Rover knowing exactly where they were going. Peter knew almost every detail of the countryside for thirty miles about.

They drove up to the old abbey where the Doctor stood outside, black and solemn with outstretched hand. When he spoke Peter chuckled at being so foolish as to think the Doctor would need translation.

'Welcome, my friends.' He shook Peter's hand. 'And may I kiss the hand of your lovely daughter?'

Flustered, Marie extended her hand and felt a strong sensation like an electric shock pass through her. They both shivered as the night calm was disturbed by a sudden gust of damp wind.

'Will you come in?' The Doctor asked in an unusually direct manner. He stood well back from the dimly lit doorway and anxiously searched their faces. It was entirely unnecessary as they casually sauntered in fully looking forward to their evening.

They were served at table by Vasaly and his new girlfriend, Thelma, both in silent and sullen mood.

'I hope you'll excuse my not eating, Mr Devereux. I'm a little unwell at present. But please don't be put off from enjoying yourselves.'

They were not. Course upon course of succulent East European dishes were brought to them. In the dim candlelit abbey they quickly developed a contented glow of satisfaction. It was considerably aided by plentiful supplies of a heavy red wine.

Marie felt unaccountably attracted to the old man. He was certainly more interested in finding out her interests than in discussing political suppression beyond the iron curtain with her father.

As they left the Doctor spoke in an agitated manner. 'Mr Devereux, since your daughter is so fond of horses why not let her come here next week when I shall have some. They will need exercise.'

Marie excitedly agreed and immediately arranged to come the following Saturday.

'Vasaly will collect you and return you to your father.'

'Thank you, that would be lovely.'

'And perhaps your father could do something for me.'

'Why, certainly,' said Peter, anxious to please.

'I have some important papers and books that certain people would very much like to get hold of. I wonder if you could store them for me. They are in a rather heavy box.'

'For you, Doctor, I should be only too pleased.'

'Splendid. Vasaly will bring it when he calls for Marie.'

They made their farewells and then Marie and Peter climbed into their car for the journey home.

'What an odd man, Dad.'

'Yes, he's very unusual.'

'No, I mean odd. Did you notice how he seemed to say so little and yet controlled the conversation?'

'Not really, dear. Though I confess I would have liked more conversation about his experience back home and especially about his escape.' He paused. 'I did notice that he doesn't seem to have seen a young girl in a low-cut dress for a long time.'

He laughed while Marie made a feeble attempt at a blush. She was rather drunk and began to ponder the merits of various boyfriends while Peter chattered away excitedly about his new friend.

'Will you tell Uncle Charles now?'

'Yes, I shall drop him a line tomorrow.'

***

At the abbey the Doctor sat quietly; saliva filled his

mouth and his pupils grew even larger as he thought of Marie and then he remembered Thelma - and the shortage of time. He retired to his room and waited. He grew more impatient as he waited on past three o'clock, past four. Then it happened.

A sudden screaming, a hoarse shouting, the patter of feet, a figure falling heavily and then a loud battering at his door.

'Doctor, Doctor, let me in. Save me please,' Thelma yelled.

Quickly he undid his latch and pushed her into the room behind him. He turned to face Ferenc who looked wild and then was suddenly cowed as the Doctor forced the big man to accept his stare.

'Go, swine. Just go.'

Ferenc slunk away grinning idiotically and Thelma clung to the Doctor in grateful thanks.

'Thank you, thank you. I was so frightened. He would have killed me.'

'Don't worry my child. I will look after you.'

He held her away from him as she clung to him in her thin nightdress. Thelma gazed up and met his eyes. He stared deeply into her as though he were penetrating her very brain. She could not look away. She tried to avert her eyes but could not. She could see only his large blue eyes staring down at her. Fixing her. She started to feel drowsy, relaxed and warm towards her saviour. He stroked her bare arms gently. Then looked down at her rapidly heaving chest. She half closed her eyes and whispered.

'Kiss me, Doctor.'

He moved slowly towards her, slowly pulled her nightdress off her shoulders. Then as he moved his head closer he took her head in his left hand, jerked it sideways and as her mouth fell open he forced his fangs deep into her neck and feasted on the warm red blood. His first for many days.

* * *

'The bloody fool. The bloody, bloody, fool' Charles Devereux roared out from his kitchen, slamming his mutton fist on the table simultaneously. He waved a letter in the air.

'Listen to this splodge of imbecility from my halfwit brother:'

> *My Dear Charles,*
>
> *You will be interested to hear that the subject of our old disputes, Doctor Kocsis, has recently arrived in this country and is living*

quite nearby.

Marie and I had a fascinating evening at his place and I have quite taken to him. I hope you will agree to meet him sometime as I am sure the confrontation will put an end to your prejudice. Marie sends her love.

Yours,

Peter

'We've got to do something Bernard. I tell you this is what we've been dreading and my ass of a brother has fallen for it. OK but its not him I am most worried about.'

'Who are you worried about then?' It was Sir Bernard, speaking gravely.

Charles looked down at his feet and shuffled.

'It's Marie. You see, she's my daughter.'

'Good God, Charles. What are you saying?'

'Oh heavens. Please keep it a secret. You see Marie was born during the war when I was out in Yugoslavia and the Balkans on missions. When my wife died I was stuck out there so Peter and his wife sort of took her over. They weren't lucky enough to have children so Peter has always treated her as his own. With my sort of job it seemed wrong to take her from them so she thinks they are her parents.'

'But why is Kocsis interested in her?'

'Oh God. I suppose this was inevitable. Listen, I ran up against him during the war. I thought he was the old "lord" type working against us but of course he works against everyone.

'I thought I'd soften him up and managed to get my wife over there as well for a dinner party. Then I realised what he really was. He attacked us both over a long period though I managed to fight him off. Dolores couldn't, and as a result of his attention she died after giving birth to Marie. Now he thinks Marie is one of his ilk. It sickens me but he has clearly come here to claim her for his own. It's up to me to stop him.'

'Are you sure of all this Charles?'

'Of course I am, damn you.'

'I'm sorry.' Bernard turned slowly and walked to the fireplace.

'For God's sake what have you come up with?' Charles roared at Roger Bentall.

'Quite a lot actually. We know for certain about a vendetta between you and Dr Kocsis caused by misplaced suspicion on both sides. It seems clear that he has come for you and of course we, that is I, will offer you state protection because of your past record.'

'But, you idiot, it is Marie who is in danger.'

'Sir my orders are to watch you.'

'All right then. I shall take charge myself. Are you with me Bernard?'

'I am your friend Charles.'

'So be it.'

***

Sir Bernard and Charles emerged from the University Library fatigued but with the strong light of determination in their eyes. As they made their way along the backs and through Kings College and its soothing stone they were silent, grim and completely resolute. The sun shone down on the crocuses and daffodils that waved a springtime greeting.

They strode to their favourite corner in their favourite pub and settled down in front of the red coals with a pint of real draught bitter each.

Sir Bernard concentrated hard to suppress a chuckle as he caught their detective, Roger, eyeing them from the other bar.

As the beer warmed his spirits Sir Bernard raised his

craggy face and touched Charles's arm.

'You know, Charles, take me as a friend and understand that I find all this very far out. I completely trust in your sincerity even after reading all that stuff.'

Charles turned. 'I know it seems crazy. But when you spend months in those mountains. Months among terrified people, months watching your wife waste away, months personally fighting a man I regard as the Devil himself.' He paused to let his voice fall. 'Then you believe. I tell you, Bernard, just you remember what happened in Holland. Now I must buy some things. I'll see you later.'

At tea time they reconnoitred in Charles's rooms. Over tea and crumpets the three worked out their strategy. Then Charles went to the phone.

'Oh Peter, it's me. Thank you for your letter. Very interesting. I should be delighted to meet this man. I've no news I am afraid, but may I speak to Marie? Thanks.'

'Hello dear, your Dad was just saying you went to dinner with Doctor Kocsis? You're going riding there? Jolly nice. When? Oh that's a pity. We bought you something I'd specially like you to have but I can't come till tomorrow. Shall I bring it then? I could drive you to Kocsis's place myself.

'He's collecting you? Oh. Well why don't I drop it in to

you there? Give me the address? Fine I'll see you there, bye love.' Charles leaped in the air and turned to his colleagues. 'Well I've got all we need.' Then he paused. 'You buggers! You've eaten all the crumpets!'

* * *

The van heaved and sighed on the bright Saturday afternoon as it rumbled up the pathway from the old abbey to the main road. Ferenc steered carefully out and drove steadily ahead. The great cathedral stood out high above the Fen and grew bigger as he came closer to his destination. At his side Vasaly fingered his stubbly chin and trembled to think of the payment for failure. He gently rubbed a spot on his chest where a red hot iron had once scorched the letter 'K' deep into his flesh.

As he daydreamed the van arrived and Marie, in full riding dress, came out to meet them.

'Nice to see you so early,' she cried. But Ferenc and Vasaly said nothing as they unloaded their evil cargo.

They grunted and sweated as they heaved the great box up the steps into the house and then into the old box room full of bric-a-brac where Peter had specially cleared a space.

An offer of tea was refused and the three drove off, Ferenc, Vasaly and Marie, looking forward to some free riding.

'Where is the Doctor?' she asked brightly.

Vasaly perked up. In his greasy way, he had realised that this was an attractive woman and he ought to ingratiate himself. 'He's asleep, but I'll take you to the horses and saddle-up.' Marie climbed aboard a beautifully built dapple grey with fine white mane and flowing tail. Just then Charles's car drew up.

'Hello, my dear. Just caught you.' He made his way slowly, noting as much detail as he could about the old abbey.

'How long are you staying?'

'About an hour, uncle.'

'Doctor about?'

'He's asleep, poor old thing.'

'Anyone else here?'

'Just Ferenc, a sort of zombie, and Vasaly, the odd job man. What did you bring me?'

'Just this my dear. I particularly want you to wear it for the next month - even at night. It's supposed to have magic properties.'

She laughed. 'You always were superstitious uncle, let me see.' She unwrapped the box. Inside was a beautiful chunky crucifix in antique silver. The huge handmade chain complemented it perfectly.

'It's absolutely gorgeous.' She flung her arms round him and kissed his cheek, warmly. 'I promise I'll wear it. Though do I really have to wear it at night?'

'Especially at night my dear.' He looked at her and turned away. Then he said softly over his shoulder, 'It's to ward off vampires.'

Charles drove off as Marie placed the crucifix and chain over her head. It rested perfectly between her breasts.

Charles soon 'phoned up Sir Bernard and Roger a few miles down the road. He quickly filled them in while they dressed for the cold damp night ahead and moved away from the road towards the Fen - towards the fields that led to the old abbey - the lair of Doctor Kocsis.

They came within sight of the building as the light began to fade. Marie was putting the horse away and then joined Vasaly and Ferenc at the van. They drove off and Charles - to his intense relief - noticed that she was still wearing the crucifix. The way was now clear.

Odd bats began to flit about as they drew closer. Roger went forward alone to see if anyone was about. He gave the all clear. Charles reached into a bag at his side. Out of it he took a large mallet and a viciously pointed stake at least a foot long.

Sir Bernard was warming to his task. I hope you're not going to use that thing old boy.'

'If I don't we and all our families are in terrible trouble. And if it helps you to steel yourself, let me tell you one more thing. Tonight is *Walpurgisnacht* - when the likes of Doctor Kocsis are at the height of their power.'

They closed in on the abbey. A lamp was soon lit and they went inside. As Charles boldly stepped from room to room the others followed gingerly.

'Ah, I've found you have I?' Charles roared.

The others hurried in to find four boxes neatly arrayed. Charles flicked the lid from the top of each one in turn to gasps of amazement mixed with relief. They were all empty. Charles laughed bitterly and flung a silver crucifix in each. 'He must be here somewhere. I must have been mad to think he wouldn't outwit me.'

Then Sir Bernard called out. 'There's someone in here.' A faint glow, as if from a candle, shone under a door. Charles motioned the others back.

Silently he pushed the creaking door open, and sprang swiftly inside. The sight before him transfixed him. He beckoned his colleagues.

The room was not stark and austere like the others. It was hung with rich purple velvets covering the entire wall space and the windows. In the centre, on a dais, stood a long coffin in perfect ebony with brass handles shining like the sun. Around it flickered a hundred candles casting shadowy light on the plush white satin lining the coffin. And inside lay Thelma in a gown of black silk which set a chilling contrast to the milk white skin of her breasts which rose in waxlike perfection over the top of her gown. Instead of the harshness of everday life her face showed the beauty of complete relaxation. This girl, who would hardly have merited a second glance in the pub, looked truly beautiful in the repose of what seemed like death.

'Good God, the poor child.' breathed Sir Bernard.

'Is she dead?' queried Bentall.

'Go on Bernard, you tell us.' said Charles, still with bitter tinge to his voice.

Sir Bernard moved forward. He was well used to assessing death. In a few moments he turned to Charles and nodded.

'How long?'

'At least a week.'

'Yet I will show you she lives,' roared Charles moving forward to Thelma's side.

'No, Charles, no,' cried Bernard in horror.

'I cannot allow this,' Bentall said springing forward to stop him. But too late. Charles turned determinedly and slammed his mallet into Bentall's face. He fell like a stone as Bernard stepped forward.

'Charles, this is madness.'

'Is it Bernard? I tell you it is necessity, to put her at peace and to allow the same to everyone else before this curse spreads across the whole country. Leave me to it before she rises before our very eyes.'

'Charles, say no more. Look,' Bernard shrilled in terrifying tones as Thelma's mouth trembled and she drew back her lips revealing sharp incisors at the corners. Charles moved forward, stake in hand. Suddenly her eyes opened, wildly casting around, but too late as Charles placed the stake on her heart and brought the full force of the mallet down.

There was a mighty scream followed by a spurt of blood as she sat bolt upright; then a despairing wail; and finally, total collapse. Charles and Bernard clutched at each other in shocked terror at what they had seen and done.

Dazedly they shuffled outside carrying the coffin. They then returned to remove the other coffins. The whole was then piled up in the garden. Charles poured paraffin over them and set an almighty blaze going.

Sir Bernard rushed in to get Bentall and found him sitting up. 'Come on Roger, we've got to get out of here fast.' They staggered out to where Charles was waiting and as the flames leaped higher they slid off. Just then Vasaly and Ferenc returned from the nearby city, with yet another girl.

As they sped along the road to Cambridge Charles, Bernard and Roger were filled with elation. 'With no coffin to return to Kocsis is finished,' said Charles. 'He will disintegrate with the coming of the morning sun. He is no more. Marie is safe.'

Sir Bernard and Roger were glad to accept this explanation. But Marie was not.

As the flames at the abbey fanned higher, her bedroom door creaked open. A soft footfall came nearer and nearer to her bed.

Marie half woke and slowly opened her eyes to find Doctor Kocsis standing over her. An expression of suffering dominated his visage as he put his finger to her lips to quash her cry of surprise.

'What are you doing here?' she whispered, her heart hammering fiercely. But as he stood averting his eyes she knew. Silently and gracefully she removed the crucifix and placed it on her dressing-table beside the bed.

He sat on the edge of her bed looking deep into her eyes. She could not help her soft hands reaching forward to hold the Doctor's tensely clenched fists. Marie struggled to calm the fires she felt within her. Fires she had never felt before and did not understand. She gently pushed her head forward onto the Doctor's chest.

What was this power he had over her? How could it be that she felt so much for this man who was older than her father? But she made no attempt to answer as she snuggled closer to the Doctor who was now stroking her head and whispering low.

'I have found you at last. Oceans and continents could not keep us apart. Nothing will ever keep me from my own,' he muttered fiercely. Marie just dug her nails into his shoulders and pulled him to her.

'Kiss me, doctor,' she whispered softly holding her head up and opening her pale lips.

The Doctor held her eyes with his searing gaze as he cupped her head in his hands and then gradually lowered his pallid face to hers. His tongue slipped into her wide open mouth and their lips pressed hungrily together.

As she sighed and moaned Doctor Kocsis slipped her nightgown from her shoulderblades.

Marie gently pushed his mouth from hers and looked into his bloodshot eyes.

'I'm ready, Doctor,' she softly said and tossed her head sideways laying bare her snow white neck.

Carefully he ran his fingers down the side of her head, down from her ear and fixed his spot. Marie clenched her teeth as his lips curled back and his incisors delicately sought their target.

She lurched violently as he entered her and they clung silently together, vampire and victim in bloody ecstasy.

It was nearly dawn before he slipped back into the huge box taking care not to disturb the label, 'Books - with care'.

'Charles and Bernard clutched at each other in shocked terror at what they had seen and done . . .'

DIES IRAE

by Richard Howard

[*RICHARD HOWARD (born 1943) is music and film critic for a provincial newspaper. He worked for some years in the film industry but abandoned it to concentrate on writing. He has long been interested in vampires and vampirism, as well as the occult in general; an interest which has led him to spend nights investigating in haunted houses and in a country churchyard reputed to be haunted - and possibly the lair of a vampire. He was honorary secretary of The Ghost Club in 1967 and 1968. His story* **Dies Irae** *is dedicated: To the many 'undead'.*]

'A well-aimed blow sent the crucifix flying from his grasp and the beads clattered to the floor...'

Like swarming ants, huddled black shapes jostled and darted against the red sunset. A few solitary figures stood away from them, looking on, and the only sound to be heard was a shuffling of feet. A moment later, out of the centre of activity, there rose a cumbersome, jagged outline. One final scurry and the moving shapes dispersed to reveal the heavy, black form of a cross, leaning slightly to one side and cutting into the brightest rays that penetrated from the distant hilltop.

Father Gerard watched from a distance as the cross slumped into the hole prepared to support it and tiny fragments of damp soil were shaken from it. Then he turned and made his way back into the old monastery to report to the abbot on the day's progress.

'Father Gerard! And what good news have you to report this evening?'

The abbot raised himself from a carved wooden chair and leant against his desk on which were strewn scrolls, papers, books, pens and a large pot of violet ink. He was a fairly tall man, more rotund than was good for his health, and with a smooth, barely wrinkled face beneath a mop of irregularly cut and slightly greying hair. His voice was more raucous than appearances led one to expect and his greeting, the same as it had been every day at this moment for years. Father Gerard sighed imperceptibly and only then seemed to gather his thoughts together.

'Work on the excavations progresses well, my Lord,' he began.

'Father Gerard, are we, in perpetuum, going to enact this daily ritual concerning address? I am, to you, Father. And you are to me. Father Gerard.'

'Very well, Father.'

'It is less formal and I am too old to need the solitude of so grand a title. You say the work goes well?'

'Yes, Father. Digging is complete and we are now at a stage for the masons to commence laying the foundations.'

'Our little community has a high standard of masonry - it always has had; the work will be complete in no time at all. You realise, Father Gerard, that this extension to our building will mean that we can enlarge our order by a substantial number of novices? I am leaving you a much enlarged community to tend.'

'As always, you talk of leaving us as if the day were already come.'

'I speak as I feel; my health could be much improved. I may not look it but I'm an old man. The community I leave behind me will not only be larger but will have considerably more potential than the one I inherited.'

Father Gerard turned and wandered to the tiny window by the abbot's desk. His lean face assumed an expression of gravity which might have been provoked by his superior's talk of failing health. Then he turned and looked towards him.

'There has been a certain amount of excitement and speculation today amongst our brethren, concerning a discovery made on the site of the new extension.'

The abbot looked inquisitive: 'Oh?'

'Late this afternoon, while digging near the edge of the proposed site, Brother Andrew unearthed a heavy wooden spar which had been buried at least six feet under the ground. He dug around it but finding it of considerable length, enlisted further help. Eventually, the entire structure was revealed to be a cross, seven feet tall. It had been lying horizontally and seemed as if it had been placed there intentionally.'

'Why do you say that?'

'Its position in the earth was completely flat. The cross itself had a small carved motif along the edges. The likelihood of such a relic's being buried for no reason at all, seems remote, but that it should have been done with such apparent care, leads me to believe that some specific purpose was intended.'

The abbot mused on what he had just heard. 'Where is the cross now?'

I told them to dig it up and erect it by the site. That was the last thing they did before work finished this evening.'

The cross looked more impressive in the early morning light than it had the night before and, as activity recommenced on the site and the masons began their task, the sheer size of the unlikely discovery, along with its decorative design, attracted much attention and provoked a certain amount of whispered speculation.

Father Gerard had just walked out to examine the relic more closely when Brother Andrew arrived, breathless, at his side.

'Father,' he began in an agitated tone, I have something to show you.'

'What's the matter, Brother Andrew? Calm yourself.'

The monk, in his excitement, tugged momentarily at Father Gerard's sleeve and hastened him away across the site, to where he had been working. They arrived at the hole where the cross had been discovered. The other monks were busying themselves on other parts of the site. Brother Andrew exclaimed and pointed down into the hole. Father Gerard's eyes widened perceptibly but beyond this, he concealed any reaction of surprise.

'It looks like a grave, Father.'

'What is so remarkable about that, my son?' he asked, glancing at Brother Andrew from the corner of his eye.

'It wasn't there last night - and now it's empty.'

'Yes, it does look like a kind of rough coffin,' conceded the Father. 'Are you sure you didn't overlook it last night?' he went on, looking into Brother Andrew's face.

'Positive! Ask those who helped me dig up the cross.'

'Have any of them seen this today?'

'I haven't shown them, Father.'

'Good. And neither shall you. Fill it in.'

The monk looked at Father Gerard in surprise.

'I mean, of course, just fill it up to the depth we require.' The Father became agitated and sensed that Brother

Andrew was contemplating an objection. He eyed the monk, reprovingly.

'Father?' asked Andrew, awkwardly.

'Yes.'

Andrew hesitated and almost decided not to continue, but finally he went on: 'The cross has caused quite a lot of speculation among our brothers.'

'Quite so. The crucifixion of Our Lord has been the inspiration for men far greater than we, to question, examine and re-examine their purposes and motives. That, surely, is why you are here today?' replied Father Gerard, deliberately choosing to misunderstand, in the hope of discouraging the young monk from further questioning. But Andrew responded, perhaps out of a certain sense of panic, by being less vague.

'What I mean, is that particular cross over there. Father.' He pointed as he spoke. 'Why was it buried here? It's big, heavy, and useless six feet under the soil. Last night, many were asking why it should be here. Speculation got the better of them all, in the end. There were many who talk of it having been put there to lay an evil spirit.

The father looked sharply at Brother Andrew: 'Is that so?' 'Some say, a vampire.'

Father Gerard looked startled at hearing the last word and was plainly surprised that Brother Andrew would bring himself to use it. He replied with emphasis: 'You know, of course, that such a thing is not possible. Therefore, do not waste your time by participating in worthless conjecture.'

'But Father, even though I laughed at them then, this grave is further proof that they might be right.'

'Proof? Vampires? Huh! Unenlightened secular superstition breeds this kind of scurrilous notion. If this is the state of the minds in our community, then the time is ripe for more invigorating and intensified concentration on our vows and lessons. Let me hear no more babble of this kind. Do you understand me, Brother Andrew?'

The monk looked sheepish: I'm sorry, Father, that I have allowed my thoughts to be distracted by the idle talk of others. But one fact remains: last night, neither I, nor anyone with me, dug deeper than was necessary to remove that cross. The grave that you see now, was still under the earth.'

It took some while for Father Gerard to decide whether the abbot should know about this latest development concerning the discoveries on the excavation site. But he concluded that the weight of a word from the abbot about the folly of superstitious gossip amongst the brothers, might be beneficial in allaying fears and dissipating any rising sense of panic. He caught himself wondering why such a reassurance from the abbot should be necessary, and then convinced himself that it would be aimed primarily at young novices who might otherwise be distracted as a result of statements made by less responsible brethren.

When the abbot heard of the new discovery and absorbed its implications, he sat back in his chair and looked for a long while at Father Gerard. 'And what do you think?'

'Above all, we must put a stop to this wild speculation about vampires.'

'Yes, Father Gerard, you've already made that plain and I shall, as you suggest, give some reassurance on that point. But having directed the minds of others towards a denial of superstition, I'd be interested to hear your own views on the subject. You tell me how such a magnificent cross came to be buried thus - and for what reason?'

Father Gerard's eyes darted from one resting place to another: 'There is no such thing as a vampire. We know that. It is true that local superstition entertains such ideas, and many more, but we know that they're bred of ignorance and fear, like all superstitions.'

'So, how do you explain the grave you tell me of?'

'There is no reason why, having dug so close to this cavity, the earth didn't simply cave in during the night.'

'Interesting.' The abbot smiled. 'But the grave was unoccupied, you say. Curious! Come, Father Gerard, are you sure that you aren't trying to fool yourself?'

'You talk as if you believe it.'

'Let us say that there are many things that we don't know. I don't know the answer to this mystery - and neither can you. I suspect that idle chatter is infectious, since you seem desperate to provide some kind of explanation to satisfy both myself and yourself. All we can do is to discourage the present rumour, we cannot offer an alternative.'

'But by not providing any explanation, however tentative, we shall only cause further speculation and be made to look ineffectual in our authority.'

'I disagree. No explanation, along with an order for silence on the matter, is preferable to a transparent excuse which will fool no one. I suggest that you make sure the Brother Andrew is silenced, by my order, and make it known that I am aware of the situation. As for the building plan, I want all attentions devoted to it and, with enthusiasm engendered, we shall simply forget about the negative occurrences of late, while directing positive devotion to the expansion of our brotherhood, in the name of God.'

Slighted at the suggestion that he had been infected by the gossip within the community, Father Gerard walked purposefully back to where Brother Andrew was working and made known the abbot's order of silence. The monk nodded his understanding.

'Have you filled in the hole?'

'Yes, Father. I did it before anyone else could see it. I have been asked why you think the cross was buried here. I told them of your disbelief in vampires.'

'Good. And remember not to mention it again.'

As the Father walked away, another monk approached Andrew: 'Well, are they taking it seriously yet?'

'He told me to say nothing more about it, to anyone/ Andrew replied.

'Then they do believe it!'

The abbot put down his pen and raised himself from his chair, muttering something as he did so. Deep in thought, he wandered over to the window which he then opened to take a breath of air. He noted with unexpected pleasure that the breeze which disturbed his study was mild, and the rustle of a few trees nearby, attracted him. His face lightened, he glanced at the half-finished sermon on his desk and decided to take a walk. Only that afternoon he had told Father Gerard that he had little or no inclination to venture out these days. Taking his cape, he passed along a stone passage and out into the garden. Beyond a high iron gate, he saw the black outline of the cross, slumped slightly to one side. Taking a key from his pocket, he let himself out of the gate and walked slowly towards the cross. It was silhouetted, much as it had been during the sunset on the evening that it was first erected, and the abbot's imagination needed no stimulating to add the detail of a human form suspended from it.

He stood next to it and laid his hand on a rough and crumbling corner. He remembered that Father Gerard had told him that the cross bore a design along its edge. He found it, facing and lit by the sinking red sun. Suddenly, something flashed across his mind. He touched the carved edge. His memory was working hard to communicate. The design extended along every visible piece of the front edge but apart from that, the cross was completely plain. Evidently it had not been carelessly constructed, and the wood used was fine quality, but time and the damp earth had badly rotted it.

The abbot looked at the design: a triangular pattern which overlapped and interlocked with a secondary, almost circular motif. It was curious and unlike anything he had seen within an ecclesiastical context. But he *had* seen it before. Suddenly it came to him. His memory broke through and he knew where to find a reproduction of just such a design.

Imperceptibly, the sun had gone from sight and the abbot had had to peer more and more at the carving to recognise the design. He blinked and realised, for the first time, the intensity of the darkness. The current rumour inside the monastery was recalled to mind and he smiled, looked quickly over his shoulder, shivered and directed himself back towards the iron gate. As he locked it, he paused once again to listen to the rustle of the trees while, in the distance, an animal cried out.

Back inside his study, the abbot hung up his cape and sat heavily down by his desk. He looked quizzically at the unfinished sentence of his sermon and brushed it aside to rummage in the tiny compartments full of all the losable objects that he had put there for safekeeping. He opened one or two of the small drawers that lined the back of the desk and his fingers lighted on the key for which he searched. He smiled as his thoughts reached the library before him and already visualised the tattered manuscript which he intended to seek out. Soon he was there too, with the glass-fronted case opened wide and a pile of torn and crumpled papers beside him. He took everything from the case, knowing exactly what he sought and, after an hour of discarding papers which he didn't want, lifted a weighty volume onto the library table. He was sure, as he peered closer, that his search had been fruitful. He was right. The edges of the front cover, bore an identical design to that which adorned the cross.

A usually particular man, he bundled the strewn

papers back into the case and locked the door. Then, excitedly picking up the large volume, he pushed it under his arm and returned to his study.

Once there, he scanned through the pages which were loose and disordered. He recalled having read much of this volume before and now, as recollection followed recollection, the dim memory of what he was really seeking, began to dawn.

The book that he was holding, contained the voluminous ramblings of his predecessor's predecessor; a somewhat eccentric abbot who had obtained his post largely as a result of his prolific sacerdotal writings. It almost seemed as if his urge to write had been compulsive, even obsessional. Amongst many theses, essays and articles, the abbot recalled that there had been a diary kept with scrupulous regularity, and it was to this that he now directed his attention.

While he searched among the multitude of loose pages crammed inside the book, he caught frequent glimpses of the motif which adorned the cover - the connecting link which had led him to the library. The design was, he remembered, an original pattern created by the writer of the book, which had apparently pleased him, and which he had used to identify and decorate many of his papers.

The abbot flicked over a page and there, staring up at him, was the beginning of a section of the diary. There was a note at the top which said that it was continued from page forty-four. He examined the page before him. It contained details of the day's services; a conversation with a young monk, Brother James, on the virtues of obedience; an account of his struggle to complete some sermons; mention of an intended visit by a bishop, whose name was illegible; and much minutiae. The handwriting was very small and neat, but it displayed several interesting graphological quirks which seemed to underline the eccentricity of the writer. Occasionally the manuscript appeared

to have been written by a decidedly unsteady hand, perhaps one feverish with excitement, anger or expectation, as in the case of the visiting bishop's name, but for the most part, it was quite legible.

The abbot pondered for a moment, as if trying to recall a particular section of the diary. He turned one or two more pages. The content was familiar but its significance eluded him. The name of *Brother Mark* seemed to leap at him from the page. There it was, underlined. He remembered now that there were incidents recorded there that related to one Brother Mark, whose name the writer abbot had *always* underlined. That was what he sought.

Taking a pen, he jotted down the page numbers on which any references to Brother Mark occurred. Large sections of the diary were interspersed with the various other contents of the book. Finally, with the diary sections located, he commenced reading. The first fleeting reference to Brother Mark was on page 75. It read:

> Today Brother Mark was received. We talked. He seems not only intelligent, but zealous - a rare combination.

The next reference to Brother Mark didn't occur until page 193:

> Father Selwyn informed me today that *Brother Mark* has, of late, been showing a distinct lack of interest towards his devotions. It seems that his former zeal has waned steadily in the past month, that he has become easily distracted and frequently displays an anguished look. Undoubtedly this latter is not due to religious passion, since he has excused himself from attending most of his obligations, including communions, on an inordinate number of occasions. This is a sudden change of heart for one who has shown great promise in the brotherhood for over a year. I have asked Father Selwyn to keep me informed of young *Brother Mark's* progress.

Then, on page 202, the abbot had devoted much space to a lengthy interview with Brother Mark, following a further report by Father Selwyn, to the detriment of the young monk. The abbot seemed to have been struck by Brother Mark's intellectual potential and even conceded an originality of mind in excess of all others within their community. This, he pointed out, was:

> ...in addition to having matured into a strikingly handsome young man whose physical excellence has been in no way subdued by the excessive plainness and simplicity of his garb and monastic environment. In fact, the effect of his surroundings serves only, it seems, to make him shine out from them, thus imbuing them, in turn, with a positive dowdiness that certainly was not intended.

The abbot smiled to himself and thumbed to the next page. He noticed that one or two other names in the diary were underlined, as well as that of Brother Mark. This fact caused him false hope, once or twice, in thinking that he had found other pages relating to the monk in question. Then he discovered a further entry of relevance:

> Father Selwyn confided to me his belief that *Brother Mark's* continuing distraction from devotion, is due to an unhealthy interest in another of our number. He dates the decline of zeal to a day shortly after the inception of eight novices. His suggestion is preposterous and I cannot accept that this over-simplified explanation could possibly apply to *Brother Mark* who, of all people, would be the last to allow such extreme reaction to be caused by an interference so minor. *If* however. Father Selwyn is correct in his belief, then *Brother Mark* must be warned about the temptations of the flesh and the value of obedience to his superior in so grave a matter. I have suggested to Father S that *Brother Mark* should be watched and I will see to it, personally, that he is.

These last remarks struck the abbot as amusing, but sad, and he flicked on to find further references to the monk. Again, the name was immediately apparent a few pages later:

> Today I concealed my presence at a vantage point near the altar in our chapel, in order better to observe *Brother Mark*. It was, however, to no avail, as I was unable to detect any action on his part for which he might be criticised. Certainly, I could not have failed to notice him among the congregation since, as I have previously stated, his intensely ambient individuality appears to permeate every corner of his surroundings. Father S has again spoken to *Brother Mark* about his apparent 'distress' and, he tells me, has offered to personally instruct and supervise him. (My wily assistant seems never to overlook an opportunity.)

Fascinated as the abbot was by these writings, he knew that there was much in this vein in the diary. His memory had almost completed the picture for him, but he was determined to find exactly what he sought and verify the facts that he believed he already knew. He therefore focused his attention several pages on, before looking specifically again for the name of Brother Mark. On page 430, he read:

> Father Selwyn is somewhat gleeful today, though he would be offended if he thought I had noticed, since he informs me that he is sure he has finally identified the object of *Brother Mark's* attraction. The monk in question is, apparently. Brother Robert (perhaps that is not so surprising). Father S claims to have seen *Brother Mark* approach Brother Robert at a moment when neither of them can have known that they were observed. Although he could not hear what was said, gestures and expressions led Father S to believe that Brother Robert was either fearful of, or offended by. *Brother Mark's* solicitation. I understand that the exchange was brief but agitated. Father Selwyn's own zeal in pursuing this... [the word 'quarry' was crossed out and substituted by 'matter'], leads me to think that his offer of personal advice and assistance to *Brother Mark* was, perhaps, over-enthusiastically declined! I have never doubted *Brother Mark's* astuteness and intelligence. In spite of that, I fear that he will find that he has thereby fallen foul of Father S.

The abbot was becoming weary but his curiosity and enthusiasm spurred him not to put aside the journal for the next morning, but to read on. Page 448 yielded the following:

> At last Father Selwyn has ceased his pretence not to gloat. In an over-excited manner, he informed me today that matters concerning the discipline of *Brother Mark* are coming to a head. He overheard the boy talking to Brother Robert and quoted the following remarks from their hasty conversation. *Brother Mark* was

heard to say: 'It is more than infatuation. I dare to admit that I am in love with you.' To which the response was lengthy: 'Dear Brother Mark. I wish I knew what to do. I am able to recognise that there are some amongst us who would go so far as to sacrifice their vows to be in my position now; you must be aware of that yourself. Believe me, I am grateful for your love, but I cannot return it in the way you need. I have thought deeply about what you have said. May God have mercy on you.' These remarks, which Father S seems to have committed to memory with a disconcerting precision, make it plain that I can rely on him to be thorough in doing *my* work. Already, I understand, he has taken *Brother Mark* aside, and, with outward friendliness, has asked him why he will not unburden himself. He even went so far as to suggest the confessional, there and then! I fear that such enthusiasm will only serve to put the boy on his guard. On the occasions of his regular confessions. *Brother Mark* has not once alluded to his emotional difficulties.

The abbot had ceased to find amusement in the pages that he now read and noted, also, the writer's increasing tendency to refer to Brother Mark as 'the boy' - a familiarity not in accordance with an abbot of integrity. His suspicion that the writer himself had a frustrated interest in Brother Mark, showed a tendency to be justified. In spite of the fact that Father Selwyn appeared as the object of the writer's jibes, there was an underlying sensation that the Father's evidently fanatical and unsubtle personality was being used as an object onto which the writer could project his own weaknesses.

On page 461, the abbot read an account in which it was plain that Brother Mark had sent a note, *via* another of the brethren, to Brother Robert. The note had been intercepted by Father Selwyn and acted as the damning evidence when, as related a few pages later, Brother

Mark was summoned to see his abbot:

> In response to my summons. *Brother Mark* today attended an interview at which Father Selwyn was also present. I questioned the boy about his numerous absences from the chapel and his inferior and inadequate approach to any task set, from simple daily domestic duties, to the sacred devotions that form his whole purpose in this community. After many inadequate responses, which added further fuel to my argument, Father S, at a nod from me, produced the note, written in the boy's hand. Although surprised, *Brother Mark* remained insolently aloof, whereupon I was forced to draw his attention to the sin of pride.

Turning the page, the abbot discovered what appeared to be the original note in question. It was a tiny scrap of tattered paper on which the handwriting, though bold in character, was faint in impression. The abbot laid it out carefully, as if strangely in awe of handling such a significant triviality. It read:

> Brother Robert, I respect your feelings and am grateful for your gentleness towards me. But I have reason to suspect that we were overheard when last we spoke together. I dread that I have led you into some kind of ill-fated association. Please be watchful, and forgive me, Mark.

The poignancy and resignation of the note provoked the abbot to pause for a moment before returning to the diary:

> Father S charged him with lustful, selfish and irreverent intent towards Brother Robert, but the boy denied all and persisted in his isolation, doggedly refusing to warm to offers of sympathetic aid from Father S and even from myself. Father Selwyn's presence might have been inhibiting to *Brother Mark*, and perhaps served only to anger him the more. One had to admire the boy's

unflinching courage in the face of so ruthless an enemy, as Father S proceeded to heap abuse and accusation on him. His face was, for the most part, impassive, even serene, but occasionally observable, was an inevitable flicker of hatred. Fortunately, Father S can easily survive such feelings - no doubt, experience has taught him how. I informed *Brother Mark* that henceforth he is to avoid the presence of Brother Robert, whenever possible, and that I expect him to make renewed efforts to establish himself once again in the esteem of the entire community, as he has already proved he can. I also instructed him to visit me in my study (every second day, to begin with) to tell me how he is progressing; I will then see about reducing the necessity of such visits. His attitude was hostile, which is regrettable, but I believe that he will change. He ventured the insulting remark, no doubt made in the heat of bitter frustration, that, with us as God's servants, God need not fear for His reputation as being all-knowing. Father Selwyn, unable to contain his venom, struck the boy across the face but appeared, nonetheless, ineffectual.

Hereafter, references to Brother Mark were invariably written in the characteristically more shaky hand, suggesting a degree of emotional involvement rather than objective detachment. There followed a list of duties and instructions for Brother Mark to observe; a list so comprehensive, that time for non-devotional thought must have been at a high premium. These additional demands, were effectual only in intensifying Brother Mark's already anguished state. Determined in their decision to force the monk into a role of obedient conformity, the plan to suppress and, hopefully, obliterate his fundamentally natural emotions, was ruthlessly applied.

The diary showed evidence that success had been obtained insofar as the regular visits to the abbot were concerned. Accounts of their conversations and the prevailing mood were recorded in every detail. The name of *Brother Mark* appeared frequently on page after page until it even began to creep into contexts where it was plainly irrelevant. In certain details, the accounts were curiously uninformative.

Reading it then, the abbot could only believe that Brother Mark's efforts towards his devotions, were pleasing his superiors. But evidence of the pressures that were being applied to him, soon became starkly apparent and an unexplained change of mood prevailed:

> *Brother Mark* today missed the evening service. I have ordered him to be placed in an isolated cell, well away from the rest of the community. His food will consist of bread and water only; and not even this on the Sabbath.

This abrupt and concise entry startled the abbot, as he shifted on his chair and moved the book into a slightly better light. Following on from the profusion of references to the monk, this entry seemed too ominous and extreme for the named transgression to be its only provocation. But no evidence was to be found of any other misconduct on the part of Brother Mark. The extreme change of mood persisted, as was plain from the now scattered, curt and isolated notes:

> After a week of solitary confinement with only bread and water. *Brother Mark* remains unrepentant. I have ordered the treatment to be continued.

And then, a few pages later:

> Repeated insolence and abuse by *Brother Mark* is reported to me by Father Selwyn. Father S suggested flogging. I agreed.

The abbot noticed that the writer had now consistently reinstated the formal address of Brother Mark throughout, although the name was still always underlined. Then the following note caught his eye:

> The flogging of *Brother Mark* seems to have taken effect. Although I did not order it. Father Selwyn saw fit to leave him in chains even after applying the whip, only allowing him the freedom of his cell in order to eat. Today I summoned Brother Robert for an interview. We discussed his development here and I suggested that he see me again in a week. A timid but pleasant boy.

This last phrase struck the abbot as the beginning of something more sinister.

References to Brother Mark were not to be found for several pages and when his name did next appear, it was with the news that he was to be allowed back to his old cell and encouraged, under supervision, to resume an active part in sacred community life. It was not clear from the diary whether Brother Mark's attitude to his superiors had changed, whether his will had been broken, or quite what had caused the decision to reinstate him. The writer abbot's interviews with Brother Robert had continued to be a frequent feature of their cloistered life and it seemed that the latter was being afforded occasional concessions and privileges.

The abbot paused to rub his tired eyes, leaned back in his chair and pondered for a moment on what he had read so far. It had been many years since he'd discovered the existence of this strange book and in the meantime, he'd almost forgotten it. Re-reading the diary, he tried to bully and cudgel his memory into informing him of the significance that it bore on the blackened wooden cross which, at that moment, stood resurrected just beyond the monastery gates. He sensed that the answer was not far away and in spite of his fatigue, he persevered into the night with these almost insanely meticulous, but revealing, jottings. The next reference was, perhaps, one of the most bizarre; the handwriting, at its most enraged:

> As instructed by me yesterday, Brother Robert took the service this evening. *Brother Mark* was allowed to attend for the first time since rejoining the community. He had been subdued all week - I believed he had learnt a lesson. Apparently not. During the service...

Here the handwriting became illegible. The next decipherable section read:

> crying out, blaspheming, threw himself at the altar, thrashing wildly, desecrating and tearing down the cross itself. His strength can only have come from the Devil. No man could propel himself to such feats when, only a week ago, he was suffering physical exhaustion. Lapsing back into his weakened state, his energy spent, he was immediately overcome and returned to the cell. God protect us from this evil.

Without doubt, the entire monastic community had been shaken to its foundations by what was plainly the act of a man who had been pushed beyond the point of no return. But hatred and fear only engendered further hatred and fear. Incensed, the writer abbot was determined to destroy Brother Mark:

> Father Selwyn came to see me this afternoon. *Brother Mark's condition is extremely weak, following the punishment meted out. I understand that he has been crying out for mercy for many hours. He is anathema. Tonight he will be excommunicated.*

On the following page, his fate was sealed:

> Today I took pleasure in visiting *Brother Mark* in his Hell. If I thought before that Father Selwyn had been over-zealous in his application of punishment, I repent of it. However, I was now stunned by the thoroughness of his methods. The creature I witnessed, bore little resemblance to the *Brother Mark* who was last seen defiling our chapel. The punishment has been eminently commensurate with the crime of sacrilege. News that he had been excommunicated was received with the most fearful groan; an anguish which conjured the torments to come. It would not have been appropriate to witness his physical expulsion from the monastery, before he had received some personal memento from me.

Again, the writing became too shaky and excited to decipher, but the entry concluded as follows:

> ...whereupon, Father Selwyn was aided in dragging him up from his cell and ejecting him from our hallowed premises. I must now take it upon myself to talk with Brother Robert, whose distress of late has been causing me some concern.

The abbot thumbed through the next few pages, surprised that there seemed to be no further mention of Brother Mark. These events, he noted, were recorded in the winter months and the survival of the expelled monk under those conditions, would be utterly impossible in his evident physical state. Somewhere, he knew that there had to be a further reference. It was inconceivable that the writer of this book would omit the fact that Brother Mark's body had been found. Having some knowledge of the extremes at which many abbot's would apply their power, he was left in little doubt regarding Brother Mark's state of health at the time he was thrown out - it was unlikely that he would have had the ability to so much as crawl out of sight. But the abbot's memory spurred him still further; it was this last entry, which he now sought, and which he almost feared to find, that would provide the key.

Scanning the pages, which now began to blur before his eyes, he suddenly caught sight of the name of Brother Mark. For a moment, as his heart pounded, he realised how caught up he had become in the fate of the young monk. The reason that Brother Mark's name had eluded him when he had scanned this page several times previously, was that it hadn't been underlined. He blinked a few times and moved closer to the page:

> Father S came to me this morning and told me that Brother Mark's body had been discovered by the edge of the wood. There was a fine layer of frost on his habit and his face. Father S seemed to be agitated and I suspected that he had been shocked by his own handiwork. However, he was so, for a very different reason. He told me that on the neck of the corpse there were two large, bloated wounds and that the body had been drained of every vestige of blood.

The abbot clenched his fist; his memory was complete. Thereafter, he easily found the passages that he now recalled having read before. The writer abbot had ordered that Brother Mark be buried, but for some reason he instructed Father Selwyn only to lay the desecrated cross from the chapel along the top of the rough coffin. Father Selwyn had suggested that a stake be driven through the monk's heart, but his superior would not hear of it. One final reference appeared at the foot of the page:

> Brother Mark has been buried outside our walls. He is temporarily at rest. I attended his funeral and...

But here the writing became shaky and illegible again. The entry ended:

> Brother Cedric, returning from an errand in the village nearby, told Father Selwyn that the people there are behaving in a curious and furtive way. There is much talk today of the howling of dogs and instances of bolting horses, frightened by something evil that passed by in the night.

The abbot now knew everything he'd wanted to discover. His thoughts drifted back to his walk earlier that evening in the dark, when he had placed a hand on the curiously carved cross. Then he relaxed and promptly fell asleep in his chair.

Father Gerard tapped briskly at the abbot's study door and received a weary response.

'Good morning, my Lord.'

'Good morning, Father Gerard' replied the abbot, not bothering to get up from his chair. 'I was reading until very late last night and I'd appreciate as little trouble as you can manage today.'

Father Gerard looked at the vast and bulging tome that was still lying on the abbot's desk. He raised his eyebrows.

'Well, Father Gerard, what is it?' the abbot enquired, a little impatiently.

I'm sorry. Father, I just came to ask you what you think we should do with the cross that was retrieved from the grave, during our excavations?'

'I have to confess that I hadn't given it much thought. What do you think we should do with it?'

'I'm not sure. This morning I tentatively suggested to some of our brothers that we should take it down and, with a little renovation, perhaps make use of it eventually in the new premises.'

'Yes. Why not.'

'However, I couldn't help noticing that there was a general reluctance to want to remove it; for the time being, at least.'

'Oh?'

'I fear that in spite of your rule of silence on the matter, our young brothers are brooding somewhat on the origins of that cross.'

'I see,' said the abbot, thoughtfully. Much of what he had read the previous night was still spinning in his mind. 'Perhaps we should leave it alone for now, Father Gerard, and then, when the new extension is complete, we'll think about employing it inside.'

'Very well, Father.'

'By the way, Father Gerard, would you ask Brother Geoffrey to see me. Thank You.'

A minute later, Brother Geoffrey was at the door: 'You wish to see me, my Lord?'

'Come in. Are you familiar with the geography of the nearby village?'

'Yes, my Lord.'

'Good. I have an errand for you.'

Work on the building progressed swiftly during that day and there was little talk to be heard on the site. Occasional calls of instruction were the only voices that broke the monotony of shuffling feet, scraping trowels and grating stone. The cross stood like a guardian, tali and gaunt, and many looked upon it as their only protection beyond the old monastic walls when dusk began to fall. The silence among so many, was unearthly; the effect was an unimaginable acceleration towards the completion of their task. As the sun began to sink behind the hill, the acceleration seemed even greater, the bustling was more flustered, movements, more brisk - the effect was mild, unspoken panic.

As the monks Anally filed towards the gates, Brother Geoffrey came hurrying from the shadows of the wood and joined the end of the silent procession. Once inside, he walked swiftly to the abbot's study and knocked on the door.

'Ah! Come in. Brother Geoffrey. Father Gerard was just leaving.'

Father Gerard hadn't been aware of it but he withdrew accordingly.

'Well, Brother Geoffrey, you found the printer I described?'

'Yes, my Lord. Here are the books,' the monk replied, putting down two newly printed and bound volumes. He was startled by what he heard next.

'Good. And what news did you hear in the village, about vampires?' The abbot's suddenly good-natured tone was difficult to interpret. The monk became flustered.

'Yes, I know, I forbade any talk of vampires. But I am entitled to waive my own ruling

What did you hear? The abbot looked straight into Brother Geoffrey's eyes.

'On no less than five occasions today, I have heard mention, in varying details, of dogs howling in the night and cringing close to their masters. One man said that he heard a tapping and scraping at his window, and even the sound of groaning, like a wounded animal, but he was too terrified to investigate it. They say that dogs were howling all-around the village until just before dawn.'

'Are you afraid, Brother Geoffrey?'

'Yes, my Lord.'

'You are safe within this monastery. If you really believe that there is a vampire, let me console you by telling you that according to folklore, such a creature can only enter a building if it is specifically invited. If you so wish, you need not go beyond our gates again. But I command you to be silent and say nothing of this to your brothers.'

As the days sped by and a profound sense of unease settled on the monastic community, the abbot began to receive further reports from the village. News came that more than one person had been laid to rest with a stake driven firmly through his heart; but never had the creature been seen.

The building plan flourished and the silent, black-clad workers moved like startled rodents around the looming cross that surveyed them. Each evening the reactions were the same. At the slightest crack of a twig, or the distant crying of an animal, all was still, ears were pricked, eyes darted, and there prevailed an unbearable sense of expectancy.

The days ran into weeks. The mood that had gripped the monks began to lose its sense of unreality and thus became their norm. The reports that came to hand from the nearby village, and now also from more distant towns, inevitably reached the ears of not only the abbot, but of every member of the community. And then, there was a certain sense of relief as the new building was finally completed and the abbot called upon to bless it. With this done and no further necessity to work beyond the walls of the community, a great feeling of peace settled over the brethren and faces dared to smile.

But that same night there was real peace for the first time in the village while, under the dim stars, a shadowy figure crawled swiftly to the top of the monastery wall, hesitated, and sped down the inside like a gigantic spider.

Dawn broke and there was an agreeable sense of satisfaction and delight in the monastery concerning the extra freedom afforded by the new premises. It was a busy day, a day of cleaning and tidying, a day for applying finishing touches. There was a general bustling that is apt to come with suppressed excitement, but only those familiar with the customs of such a community would have been aware of what was happening. The abbot received word that a dozen new novices would be arriving within the week. Letters were despatched, consultations held and plans prepared.

It was late that evening before Father Gerard found a moment to make his daily report to the abbot. Walking along a narrow stone corridor, he happened to glance down as he passed a flight of descending steps that led to one of the many cellars. It was an ill-lit passage, but in that fleeting glance, he was certain that he caught sight of a figure as it passed from view into the darkness on the curving steps. Although he had been hurrying, he paused for a moment and watched. A draught stirred a cobweb that was suspended in the gloom halfway down the steps, and he felt cold. He was puzzled that anyone should be going down to the cellar at that particular moment and since, anyway, they carried no light, he decided that after a busy day, his mind had played a trick.

But the next morning, Father Gerard learned that his was not the only mind that had taken to trickery, and something very unusual was happening in the monastery. No less than three monks confided to him early that day that they had seen a cowled figure roaming the passages of the building, and in one instance, when the witness had gone in pursuit, the figure had glanced over his shoulder before rounding a corner and fleeing towards the cellars. In that brief moment, the monk, a middle-aged man who had spent many years in the brotherhood, failed to recognise the dark and half obscured features as belonging to any of his fellows.

During the service of that evening, the abbot, having chosen to attend, occupied a chair set to one side of the congregation. He had ordered, the previous day, an elderly brother to conduct the ceremony and began to wish he hadn't as the voice droned on and tended to lull him to sleep. His eyes roamed about the chapel, of which every corner was familiar in detail, and resorted, ultimately, to counting the rows of monks, in order to occupy his attention. Narrow, stone pillars effectively partitioned off the carved wooden pews occupied by the monks. Drowsily, after yet another active day, his mind totalled the figures as the sixty cowled monks knelt in prayer.

After the service, Father Gerard went to the abbot's study. He didn't wait for the customary greeting but launched into his speech straight away.

'Father, I'm afraid I have some rather disturbing news to relate.'

The abbot's face looked questioningly at Father Gerard and he gestured for him to continue.

It is simply that I have heard three reports today, of a stranger in our midst who roams the monastery at night. Our brothers are becoming very disturbed and, unfortunately, I was not in time to stamp out the rumour before it became common belief. In fact, Father, I have to confess that I think I too have seen this apparition. It was when I was coming to see you at this time yesterday and as I was feeling rather exhausted, I dismissed it as something from my imagination.' Father Gerard's voice was becoming shaky and breathless.

'Sit down. Father Gerard. I spoke once before about popular rumours being infectious and I perceived then that you were slightly offended. Dare I suggest that this is a recurrence of the same phenomenon?'

'I'm sorry, Father, you're probably right.'

'Perhaps.'

'If you'll pardon me for mentioning it. I've always tended to think that you entertain the possibility of some truth in this not so distant rumour of a vampire.'

The abbot smiled: 'And you think that there is a connection between this latest rumour and the one that we have only just managed to quell, concerning vampires?'

Father Gerard began to feel that he was being foolish and decided to change the subject. He coughed. 'Oh, I almost forgot. Brother Anthony is feeling unwell and asked me to convey his apologies for not being in attendance at the service this evening.'

At first, the significance of this simple statement didn't fully register with the abbot, but then his mind posed a question. He began rather absent-mindedly: 'Thank you for telling me. Father Gerard, how many were in attendance?'

'There should have been sixty but of course there were only fifty-nine on this occasion.'

There was a pause.

'I counted sixty.'

'Oh, then...'

They exchanged glances.

'I wasn't mistaken. There was ample time to count and recount, which I did. I see I must be frank with you, Father Gerard. You are correct in supposing that I have given credence to tales of vampires; in fact, I have evidence. You must have heard the stories that filtered in here from the village. Can all those be wrong, and we right? Men don't bolt their doors against nothing. Perhaps one or two will, but you cannot ignore and deride an entire village that does just that.' The abbot got up and walked to his desk: 'The facts are in this book, if you care to read it. The vampire, unleashed by us, was once resident within these walls. It is perhaps natural that he would want to come back for vengeance.'

'Vengeance?'

'He has much to avenge. But there are things that I don't understand. How did he get in here?'

'And how, anyway, could a vampire survive on hallowed ground? And why would he attend a religious ceremony?' 'There is much that we don't know. The folklorists themselves seem to know little and are frequently in conflict. They contradict not only each other, but even themselves. I will give it thought tonight. Come to me first thing in the morning. Good night, Father Gerard.'

That night, a rending crash shattered the silence that had settled over the now, once again, uneasy community. The sound came from the direction of the chapel and panic spread swiftly from cell to cell. The abbot had been lying awake, deep in thought, and physically jolted at the suddenly ominous sound. He scrambled from his bed and, snatching his cape, hurried along to the chapel. Monks were already hovering around the corridors and Father Gerard came running from the opposite direction.

Several people converged at the same moment on the two chapel entrances. The sight that greeted them caused shock and terror. Oaths were uttered and some of the monks reached states of near hysteria. Standing on the altar was Brother Anthony, tearing down the draperies and destroying anything that came to hand. On the ground was the vast crucifix that had replaced the one of previous generations, and it was the shattering of this which had roused the sleepers.

The abbot shouted an order and he and Father Gerard were the first to reach Brother Anthony. Brother Geoffrey threw himself at the defiler's ankles and brought him down. His head cracked against the marble altar and he was still. Monks crowded around and then a silence fell as Brother Andrew exclaimed: 'Look! His neck!'

Father Gerard, grabbing Brother Anthony's head by the hair, turned the neck to full view. Two fresh, bloated wounds oozed blood which trickled onto the marble slab. Now was acknowledged to all, not only the existence of the vampire, but its presence within their midst.

In the remote hope of allaying panic, the abbot briskly shouted for the monks to assemble within the chapel, where, after a brief consultation with Father Gerard, he would address them. He ordered three of the brothers to go and make sure that none remained in their cells and to assemble the entire population of the monastery. Then he motioned to Father Gerard to join him in his study. With the Father close at his heels, he hurried back and closed the door behind them.

'Father Gerard,' he began urgently, 'this is not a time for seeking answers to our former questions. The facts are plain and we must deal with the situation here and now.' He suddenly clutched at his chest and wheezed violently. Father Gerard helped him to a chair.

It took a minute for him to recover, before he was able to continue: 'A thorough search must be organised and carried out now. We have enough brothers for such a task to be possible. Concentrate on the cellars. There's a maze of passages, vaults and cells beneath here and every one must be searched.' 'Wouldn't it be better to wait until morning?'

'It's barely midnight now. In those five or six hours, anything could happen. Arm yourselves with whatever you like. Anything! But I want him found. Those marks on Brother Anthony's neck mean that he too will live on as one of the undead - a vampire - unless we bury him with a stake through his heart. How many more of our brothers must suffer this fate if we delay tonight? No. I want it done now. And you will help. You will lead the search, delegate responsibilities, choose those you can best rely on to subdue panic and encourage the fainthearted. I would do it myself if I had strength enough to get as far as the chapel. Now is your hour. See to it. Prove yourself.' The abbot gave a dismissive gesture and gasped to catch his breath.

'One question, my Lord.'

'Yes?'

'What made Brother Anthony desecrate the chapel?'

The abbot replied more softly: 'In legend, the vampire can hypnotise his victims. That is why they return and allow him to drink more of their blood. Terrified as they are, they cannot resist, and it is only when they die through loss of blood, and are buried without being laid to rest according to that legend, that they too rise again as vampires.' He paused. 'Be cautious. Father Gerard.'

As the Father's footsteps faded away along the stone corridor outside, the abbot slumped back in his chair and sighed. Whether, for a brief moment, he fell asleep, he was unable to tell, but the next thing he realised was that his study door clicked shut and the key was being turned in the lock. Before him, across the room, stood a figure wearing a monk's cowled habit. The abbot started, blinked violently and made an inarticulate noise. The figure turned towards him, lifted its head and walked a few paces across the room. The abbot peered at the shadowy face which was only half visible beneath the cowl. Then, to confirm his most dire suspicions, he realised what was missing - no crucifix hung from the neck of this monk. The figure raised its bony hands and threw back the cowl.

'They won't find me, Abbot.' The voice was hard and bitter and came from blood-flushed lips, set in a young and god-like face of shadowy marble. Black hair curled about his head and everything that the abbot remembered reading, began to make sense.

'Brother Mark?'

'Once it was so.'

'And now?'

'One of the many undead.'

'How did you get in here?'

'You invited me; by choosing to build around my grave.'

'And what do you want of us? Is it revenge?'

'I want blood. Let us say that I foresaw an opportunity. There are more tunnels and rooms beneath this building than any of you know. I spent much time down there, many years ago. Your friends will be gone for hours.'

'But how can you survive here, in a religious environment?' 'It is a temporary measure. You might as well ask, how you can be close to a fire. Only if you touch it, will it burn; otherwise it will simply keep you warm.'

'I know your weaknesses. Brother Mark. You're vulnerable.' 'You're not the first abbot to tell me that. We are all vulnerable.'

The abbot looked straight at Brother Mark, whose eyes burned like coals and fixed him with an unblinking stare. There was a momentary silence.

'What happened to you, Brother Mark, after your note to Brother Robert was intercepted by Father Selwyn?'

Brother Mark flinched at the mention of these names. The abbot went on: 'You were ordered to visit your abbot each second day, were you not?'

Again Brother Mark's face contorted slightly and he showed surprise that the abbot knew about his past.

'The abbot,' he spat, 'knew everything about me, and he exploited it. He was an insanely jealous and frustrated man. At first I tolerated his abuse, yielded to him and bargained my way through life, because I knew that if I didn't, my existence would be a hell. But it became too much. I weighted one hell against another and one day I defied him in the way he least expected. I fear that Brother Robert suffered for that.'

'What happened?'

'He demanded more and more. He promised absolution in return for favours. He became obsessed with me. And the more he tried to love me, the more I despised him. The day I lashed out, he had me confined. And every day, he visited me, chained me and told me how much he loved me. Even on the night he excommunicated me and threw me out, he declared his love. He, and his world, everything it stands for, you, and all the others like you, you are hypocrisy personified. You create us, and then you are the first to condemn us.

'Us?'

'Yes. The undead.'

'Your present state is not the work of your abbot. I've read his diaries. I know what led up to your expulsion.'

'They threw me out. They harassed me and beat me, they denied me food so that my body was weak and I became ill, they tortured and mangled my emotions, and then, as if that weren't enough, they cast out my spirit into blackness, as they did, my body. I was physically, mentally, emotionally and spiritually vulnerable, and it was their work. I am what I am because of them. One such as you, damned me.'

The abbot began to mutter in Latin and finger the crucifix that hung about his neck. As he did so, Brother Mark picked up a heavy candelabrum. The abbot pushed himself to his feet. A well-aimed blow sent the crucifix flying from his grasp and the beads clattered to the floor. The candelabrum landed heavily against the abbot's chest and winded him. He fell.

The abbot stirred and, with an ache in the chest, lifted himself from the floor. Brother Mark was sitting close by and immediately stood up.

'Look at me,' he ordered. And the old man was transfixed by the hypnotic stare. 'Sit down, Abbot, and listen to me carefully.

Your brother monks will be gone until dawn unless they are summoned. Shortly we shall go and ring the bell for service. It can be heard plainly in the subterranean cells, I assure you. Whatever confusion this might inspire, it will inevitably bring your Father Gerard running here. I shall be interested to meet him, and you will introduce us. As your personal assistant, he will be a necessary part of our plan. After we have been introduced, you will announce that you have evidence that the vampire has fled from the monastery. You will assure your entire community of this fact and proclaim a special full mass and communion tonight, to offer prayers and supplication for deliverance and peace. Prior to the service, the brothers will be ordered to retire to their cells, from whence they will be summoned, one by one, to be received in the secrecy of the confessional by you. It will be a simple matter to initiate each brother in turn. By morning, the task will be complete and the brotherhood will commence devotions of a different kind.'

Brother Mark made a gesture and the abbot, fully conscious of what he had been told, emerged from the trance.

'Well, Abbot, I think you understand me now. It's curious that even after everything I underwent in this monastery, that hypocrite couldn't bring himself to mutilate my body with a stake. He must have known that one day, even if the cross that he placed on my coffin had not been removed, it would simply have crumbled away and I would have returned.' Brother Mark pulled the cowl about his head. 'And now it is time to ring the bell.'

The abbot lifted his hand to a sudden stinging sensation on the side of his neck. He touched it and winced. Blood, coloured his fingers.

'Fasten your collar. Abbot. Everything must be perfect for our special communion.'

MIRROR WITHOUT IMAGE

by James Turner

[JAMES TURNER is the author of sixteen novels, five columns of poetry, books on eccentricity, martyrdom and topography. He has edited five anthologies and written a two-volume autobiography. He has lived in several haunted houses and, at one time, owned and lived on the site of Borley Rectory, known as 'the most haunted house in England'. He was born in Kent, lived for twenty years in East Anglia, moving to Cornwall in 1959 where the natural surroundings contribute an important element to his poetry and frequent broadcasts and TV programmes. He is a member of the BBC Advisory Council for the South West of England.]

'The utter transformation of her features was horrible . . .'

Parts of Suffolk are very remote indeed. Small communities are to be found separated from each other by what pass for roads, little untrodden ways beside dark brooks and even darker millpools no longer used. To those who know them these paths are well-defined and lead through plantations of bat willows, up into the park of some forgotten mansion, or to some outlying farmhouse the lights of which sometimes stream across a ploughed field at night.

Even in summer such paths have their familiar phantoms. Past evil lingers still. That freshly turned heap of earth just within the wood where the brambles have been cut back, what lies beneath it? And how came what lies beneath it to be there at all? In winter, if you pass that way, perhaps upon the heap of earth will stand the wraith of a child. Or will it be no more than the mist rising from the valley, from the water meadows, where nothing grows but skeleton reeds rustling with every breath of wind? Time, in such places, has stood still. When you turn off the highroad and go into the lane, you enter a place quite different from the usual idea of 'country'.

The hamlet you arrive at is nothing but a collection of sordid cottages and a massive, rotting church. With exceptional luck an inn will lie beside the lane, with low ceilings, oil lamps and smoky fires. A midden will be at the back door, with chicken and pigs rooting. At cottage doors stand old crones with ugly faces and twisted bodies and memories going back into the past, great ageless racial memories of children sacrificed to pagan gods, of things which lie buried beneath freshly turned earth within the wood edge. Upstairs, behind the tiny, never-opened windows, on an ancient bed, will be a thing which was once a fair girl, which has lain there for twenty years, mouthing inanities and slobbering.

What hidden secrets shall not such a creature have, of bats with men's eyes which flew in, fifty years ago, and deranged the girl at her mirror, before feasting on her blood? These cottages stretch back to the days when Pan himself was seen in the spinneys: when electricity cables did not run across the country; and there were no proper roads at all. Those who live here are the last to hold the knowledge of that language which is Time's great secret. When they are gone who shall inhabit the lonely dwellings?

***

The mill house, which I had rented a year ago in order to concentrate on a novel I was writing, lay in such a hamlet, at one end of a valley. About three miles away stood Landred Hall. I had met Mrs Hedingham, who owned it, at a dinner-party in London. She had, then, invited me to come to Landred whenever I wanted. And, although I had seen Pauline, her daughter, once or twice, riding up the valley on her grey horse, it was not until today that I had been to the hall.

I left my home (which stood just a little above the floor of the valley) by the front gate beside the ruined mill itself. I struck off through the woods where, in winter, the hunt came down the hill into the lane, and crossed the open space into the first of the trees. So, in a little while, I came out on the raised rampart of earth forming one side of the now disused mill-stream and walked to where the brook, coming down a tiny ravine, turned left and wandered off through the water meadows. Today it was very shallow.

The afternoon was one of the most peaceful I can remember. The sun was falling through the leaves of hazel bushes, a white cow moved a few feet deeper into the buttercups, the lark dropped to earth. I turned the corner where the brook came out from the trees into open country, what would have been grazing land if anyone had bothered to look after it. Now it was nothing but a tract of stunted thorn bushes and scrub. A jay screamed away ahead of me; a turtle dove sighed itself into a summer sleep from the top of a pine tree; the world (or at any rate my portion of it) was very lovely.

When I began to go up the sloping field I could see the roofs and chimneys of Landred Hall in the distance. Perhaps if I had turned back then things would have been different. I do not know. I had walked this way a hundred times and every time it was different. But, since I had never gone as far as this I was not ready for the change in the landscape. Where before all had been wilderness and the confusion of nature, here the land, the park meadows, the trees and the spinneys were looked after and cared for. Sheep were grazing under the elms and the park itself was wired to keep them in. Across the wide lawns was the house itself basking in the sun.

So, for the first time, I came to Landred Hall, that Georgian house built on the foundations of a much older Elizabethan mansion. I had hardly set foot on the gravel path before Mrs Hedingham - whom I later came to know and love as Beatrice - came out from the french windows of the library and greeted me. 'Mr Brook,' she said smiling, holding out her hand. 'How nice of you, how very nice!'

I had never, when I thought of coming to Landred, imagined it would be like this. 'I do hope,' I said, 'that you'll forgive my coming over unannounced. My telephone is out of order and it's such a beautiful day.'

'But nothing could be nicer,' she said and added almost with a note of alarm (but not explanation) in her voice, 'I believe I would have come to you had you not come to me.'

We crossed the lawn and sat down beneath an ancient mulberry tree in chairs arranged round a wooden table.

'We, more or less, live out here in summer,' she went on, talking nervously and a little too quickly. I said how delightful it was actually to be sitting in the garden of a house I had so often glimpsed from the edge of the wood. What struck me as odd then, and still does, is that Beatrice confided in me, though we had not been together for more than ten minutes. It was almost as if she had expected me.

'I believe,' she went on, 'that I've only two interests in life. No, three. Landred is one of them, Pauline, my daughter and poetry are the other two.' And when I did not reply at once she added, jumping up, 'Come and look at the house. I love showing it to friends.'

I think Beatrice is the only person with whom I have ever been quite at ease in so short a time. The grace of her movements, the loveliness of her voice and her intelligence, were a joy. She was very fitting to own such a beautiful house. And, indeed, I can remember very little of the interior as we passed from one room to the next. Was I already in love with her?

But I do remember vividly how we came up a short flight of stairs and into an empty attic. She laid her hand on my arm and took me to the window. She brushed away the cobwebs from the glass. 'Look,' she said, 'I want you to see it from here. Over there.'

I looked in the direction she was pointing and saw, cleaving the air, what looked like an enormous tooth upside down, with its fangs raised.

'It's what's left of a castle and a moat,' she went on, 'maybe dating from the thirteenth century. Just that one pile, the eastern gate. It's part of the Landred estate.' And with that she suddenly went from the window, across the attic and out of the door. The spider she had disturbed began again to weave its web over the window pane.

I stood for a moment, looking at the ruin, wondering why she wished me to see it. I came to the conclusion that she was in some sort of trouble and needed my help. And this trouble was connected with the castle ruin. I turned to ask her but she was gone. Up here, under the boughs of trees pressing tightly against the house, it was cold and damp, even today. Quickly I shut the door after me and went down the stairs to where she was waiting.

'I'm sorry,' she said, leaving you like that. Believe me, it wasn't bad manners, really it wasn't. I wanted you to be alone a moment with your first view of the castle.' She raised her hand 'Have patience with me and before you go, and after you've seen one other thing, I will explain.'

I knew then that she needed my help. When I followed her, once more, out of the french windows on to the lawn Pauline, her daughter, was sitting in one of the chairs under the mulberry tree.

'Darling,' Beatrice said. I knew she had checked herself from running to the girl. I could feel her body stiffen beside me. I could sense that when she saw her daughter she forgot that I existed. 'Darling, I didn't think you were coming back until later. You haven't tired yourself walking in the sun, have you?'

Pauline sat very still, looking past Beatrice, at me. And although she said, 'As a matter of fact, mother, Elaine met me at the station and brought me home,' she was not really aware of what she was saying. She was looking at me with an almost savage, feline look on her beautiful face. For beautiful she was in the way a statue is beautiful and, at the same time, pale and ill-looking as if she had been carved out of marble. Our eyes met. In that second I knew that she would kill me if she ever got the chance. And then Beatrice took my arm and broke the hypnotism of her daughter's eyes.

'Pauline, dear, this is Mr Brook,' she said, her fingers trembling in mine. 'He lives quite near, at the old Mill House. We met in London.'

Pauline, whatever she saw in me, controlled her terror by suddenly leaping from her chair. I was sure then, that in me she saw an enemy who could destroy something with which she was so much in love that she would not have hesitated to kill to preserve it. She appeared, also, to be sleep-walking and her words when she said, 'I believe I've seen you, Mr Brook, passing through the woods on the other side of the lake. Has mother been showing you the house?' were dull and spoken only with a compulsion of manners.

'Yes. It's really lovely,' I said, 'I envy you such a home.'

'Elaine says the same thing. She loves the house because it has a history, because it's so English.'

Beatrice turned to me. 'Elaine,' she said, 'is my only tenant.' And then to Pauline. 'Why on earth didn't you ask her to stay here, my dear?'

'I did ask her,' Pauline snapped, 'But she has a lot of new clothes and I've promised to go over and help her alter them. As a matter of fact, I ought to be going over now.'

'But, Pauline, you look so tired. Why don't you rest a little and go over tomorrow? There can't be all that hurry.'

And, indeed, the girl did look ill. I fancied she needed a great effort to drag her body across the lawn to the house. 'I'm quite all right, mother, really. I must go. I promised Elaine.'

When she pronounced the word Elaine her eyes shone with a light quite belying the obvious lassitude of her body.

'I do wish you'd take more care of yourself, my dear. You'll be in no condition to enjoy your birthday party next week.' 'Oh, do be quiet, mother.' Pauline rasped out, flinging her hands up in irritation. 'You've always disliked Elaine. I don't know why.'

She left us then and went through the french windows.

I got up as she walked away and saw, when she crossed the threshold, that she leant against the table inside as if she could not go another step without its support. I took a pace towards the door in order to catch her if she fell. She must have been aware that I had seen her weakness for she pulled herself up and turned to me with such a look of hatred in her eyes that I was unable to face her. I went back to my chair under the mulberry tree. Beatrice had not moved.

'Was,' I asked, 'your daughter's state of weakness the other thing you wanted me to see?'

I think it was that question that decided her to open her heart to me. 'Not here,' she whispered. 'Not here. We will walk down to the lake and through the wood. I don't understand how it is you could be sure that Pauline was the other thing I wanted you to see. Have you any idea of the danger she's in?'

We had reached the end of the long lawn sweeping down under the magnificent beech tree to the lake. A moorhen flustered across the still surface and disappeared into some reeds. When the ripples made by its feet subsided there was a deep stillness in that part of the garden.

'I believe I have,' I said. 'Obviously, of course, your fears for Pauline are connected with her friendship with Elaine who, I assume, lives in the castle?'

'Yes. It was why I wanted you to see it. Pauline brought her here one day last year, from London. About this time.' She broke off a leaf of a briar rose growing at the edge of the water and began twisting it in her fingers. 'She said, Elaine that is, that she fell in love with the place the moment she saw it. She said she felt she had come home and begged me to let her the ruin and that, if I did, she would have it put into some sort of order, enough to live in. I did it for Pauline's sake. Now, alas, I only wish I'd never let her have the place.'

'But have you any proof that Pauline is under her influence?' She turned to me quickly, throwing away the rose leaf. 'Look at Pauline. There's proof enough. She's ill, uncivil and completely changed. Poor darling, it's not her fault. But I'm convinced that she'll die if I don't do something. Oh, Mr Brook, is there anything you can do?'

'Do you think she might be getting drugs to Pauline?'

'No. I should say the reverse. Pauline used to be so happy and full of life. And that is exactly the point. She is herself again at specially defined periods, when she is away from Elaine. Then she overcomes this weakness, her body regains its old strength. It's almost as if blood returned to her veins. And then something happens, something terrible I'm sure, and she becomes pale and listless like you saw her today.'

'It's no good forbidding her to see Elaine?'

'I've tried. I only made things worse. She threatened to leave home altogether and that would have been the end. I can, at least, help her a little while she still comes home.'

'And doctors?'

'What use are doctors if her life is threatened as I think it is? They wouldn't understand. I hoped you might.'

By this time we were past the lake and walking down a

long grove of fir trees into which the sun scarcely penetrated. Before us was the monolith of the castle ruin on its mound of green grass. As we watched the figure of Pauline, in a white open sport's shirt and blue skirt, ran up the slight hill and pulled at the massive wooden door. In a moment the door had shut behind her and we, watching from the wood, were left with the utter stillness of evening.

'Unbelievable as it is,' I said, now much surer of my ground, 'I think I'm beginning to understand. What is Elaine like?' 'Like? Well, she's beautiful, I suppose. She doesn't spend a great deal of her time here. She's mostly in London. But whenever she does come Pauline is here. I remember, once, last autumn, Elaine had been in London and Pauline was in France with some friends. The very night Elaine returned Pauline arrived back, though her holiday was not due to end for another week.'

'Did she say why?'

'Only that she was bored with Paris. From that evening she became ill again until, well, until Elaine was gone. Do you think I'm wrong to connect the two of them in this way?' 'No, you're absolutely right. And I think it may be extremely dangerous and horrible. But you haven't told me what Elaine is like, have you?'

'That's the odd part. Now you ask me to describe her I don't seem able to. She has black hair. And once, when I shook hands with her, a greeting she appears actively to dislike and avoids most of the time, her hand seemed unnaturally cold as, you'll think me quite mad, as though she wasn't living at all but was a corpse walking.'

***

When Pauline spoke of her birthday party she really understated the affair. The whole of Landred Hall was given over to its celebration. The evening itself was set with a flaming sun, the light of which had not died when I drove through the thousand fairy lamps lining the drive from the main gates to the house, and went through the open front door into the stone-flagged hall. In a way, so skilfully was the work done, the garden looked like an extension of the house. Guests were already overflowing on to the lawns and into the large marquee there.

Pauline, once again herself, was excited with happiness. She flung herself into the arms of one partner after another and never seemed in the least tired. Elaine must have been merciful. Yet I knew that the reason that Elaine had left her alone for over a fortnight, which had allowed her to recover, was myself, unless Elaine could deal with me there would be no peace for her.

'Charles,' Beatrice said as we stood together at a window watching the scene. It was the first time she had used my Christian name. 'I could cry with pleasure to see Pauline her old self. When I look at her tonight I begin to think her illness was nothing more than some sort of adolescent weakness and that she is over it.'

'You must not think that,' I entreated. That is exactly what Elaine wants you to think.'

'You mean...?'

'I mean she has only temporarily relaxed her hold on Pauline. Such things as Elaine are, never let their victims go. They can't.' I felt Beatrice shudder and draw closer to me. I looked up and standing before us, her long evening dress touching the floor, black and with the smallest medici collar of stiff lace, her black hair tightly drawn from her forehead and done in coils at the back of her head, was the most commanding figure of a woman I have ever seen. I had not expected Elaine (for it was she) to be so tall. I had not expected her to have, in her bearing, the look almost of majesty.

'Elaine,' Beatrice went to her and there was, in her voice, a special note of pleading. 'Elaine, my dear, I'm so glad you've come. You must see Pauline in that dress. How good of you to give it to her, it's quite made her birthday for her. Now come and let me introduce you to Charles, Mr Brook, a great friend of mine who lives close by.'

When she moved towards me the air of the summer night grew colder. Or so I imagined. I was amazed that Beatrice did not notice it. The band, at that moment, was playing a waltz, a long, drawn-out, sickly melody. I looked up into those eyes and saw, as I had known all along that I should see, not the eyes of a woman, but of some animal, some trapped and haunted and fear-stricken animal about to strike at something come to kill it. I knew (for the change in her eyes was but for that second and for me alone) that we were enemies, that the hatred with which Pauline had first met me was nothing compared with that before me now. I suddenly shivered with fear. A moment later her eyes had returned to human shape and she was smiling.

I knew I was being warned. In order to cover my confusion I offered to fetch her a drink. When I returned with the champagne she was sitting on the terrace. I sat down beside her, my courage returned. 'Don't you think Pauline looks lovely tonight?' I asked and raised my glass to drink. Her eyes over the rim of her glass were gazing at me and I knew, then, where her power over Pauline lay. If I did not take care it would not be with Beatrice that I was in love.

'Why have you come to Landred?' she asked. The anger in her voice vibrated between us. And when I did not answer, for what, indeed could I answer since I had never seen her before, though her question implied that she recognised me, she went on. 'Go away and don't come back. Don't ever come back, or meddle with affairs which don't concern you.'

'What makes you think I've the least desire to meddle, as you put it, in anyone's affairs?'

'I heard your words to Beatrice, "Such things do not let their victims go". Are you such a fool as to imagine that I don't already know all about you? I who have been...'

The smile on those lips made me want to put my hands to her throat and crush the life out of her. If life it was which was directing her? I blurted out, 'When this is over, Elaine, one of us will no longer be alive. You cannot make me go away.' I could not believe that this person who called herself Elaine was not flesh and blood like Beatrice. Of course, then, under the fairy lamps, she was flesh and blood, real and yet cold with the aged cold of the grave in her.

'You are in love with Beatrice?' she asked the question to which she needed no answer, for she had known love - and hate - for centuries. They were no mystery to her.

'Even if that's true,' I said, 'it's of no consequence. It is not a matter between us. Between us is only life and death. Love does not enter into it.'

She laughed a little low laugh. 'Don't be too sure,' she said, 'I could make you kill yourself with love for me. Like the knights of old I could command you even unto death. It would not be the first time and it would be amusing to try, to take you from Beatrice, to make you sick for me.'

'As you have done with Pauline?'

She flared up then. She swung round at me. 'Leave her out of it,' she almost spat the words. 'Listen to me now. Go away, as I've told you to, and while there is yet time. I've no wish to harm you.'

'But,' I said, looking away from her and her hatred. 'But I am different. You cannot do as you please with me because I have recognised you for what you are, and because I do not come unguarded. Because my love for Beatrice will defeat your death.'

'You are no different.' She was contemptuous. 'All the others have been interfering fools. They died. What can you know which they did not?'

'This,' I spun round on her, 'that you are alive but for a moment. That without Pauline, or some other, you are dead. Your proper place is back there with the others, in the vaults. You are the living shadow of a dream.'

What courage dared me to speak so to her, I do not know. She raised her right hand. The light was so dim that I could see no more than the burning red of her animal's eyes and hear the hissing of her breath. When she turned upon me to destroy me I swung round and held out my hand. There, in the palm, shining in the reflected light of the fairy lamps, lay the silver crucifix with which I had armed myself.

She turned and fled and was gone into the summer night. I knew I had only made it more dangerous for Pauline - and myself.

***

She made one mistake. All her magic, which was undoubtedly powerful, was destroyed by it. She should have come straight to the door of my cottage and taken me unawares. As it was she chose to stand beneath the fir trees in the path leading down to the valley and to Landred. She must have forgotten that it was probable that I should be watching from some window in the house. As it was she nearly defeated me. Yet I had time to fetch my further protection.

That she could command certain midnight powers, that the very blood in her veins was, in some horrible way by means of her daughter, the same as Beatrice's, did not make the struggle a foregone conclusion. With Elaine I was not dealing with a being any longer capable of pity. She was not a being like myself, like Beatrice, like Pauline, even if she lived on the girl. She was altogether different whatever disguise she chose to wear. And I knew that, for her, time was running out.

As I watched the figure by the tree I began to hear the siren call, the soft, magical music by which I knew she was able to call Pauline to her. And now she was calling me. She would come, surrounded by the magic of her song, would have what she needed of me. When she went I would be dead and she engorged with my life. No one, the next morning would have the least idea how I died. They would speak of heart attack, not knowing that every drop of my blood would be racing in Elaine's body.

I watched her move slowly, floating almost on the white mist about her feet. I think I could have cried out with relief when I flung back the door and found I had been wrong, that it was not the black-haired Elaine who was standing there but Beatrice herself. I took her by the hand and led her to the sitting-room.

'I had to come,' she said. 'Pauline has gone across to some friends and Landred seemed so lonely. Will you forgive me?' She slipped off her light summer coat and helped me to make coffee. 'You should have asked me to come over,' I said, 'Not come along the valley at this time of night alone.'

'Oh, that's nothing. I like the night and the mist in the brooks. Besides it's not late really. After all I've known these parts all my life.' She shook her golden hair and laughed happily. 'If you insist you shall show me home,' she added. 'Isn't it exciting to think that we're in a small world of our own and that no one has any idea at all that we're here together?'

Even before she had uttered the last word I had taken her in my arms. 'Beatrice,' I whispered, 'I love you. You must know I've loved you from the first time I met you in London. Do you remember?'

'Charles.' Her hands were at each side of my head. There was a sudden comfort in holding her body in my arms and feeling her hands fall to my shoulders and so about my neck. When she lowered her head I put my hand into her golden hair where she had let it fall down her back. I was overcome with erotic joy for her. I surrendered myself without a thought. I felt her hands, with exquisite sexual delight, come about my throat - and was lost.

She forced me backwards on to the couch. I could feel the strength of her passion in her hands and fingers which were no longer fingers but claws beginning to tear at the side of my throat. And still I was unaware of her deception; still I longed for her body; for her mouth to tear my flesh; to be absorbed into her erotic cruelty. Now, in her frenzy, she was tearing at my clothes. I was drowning in the heat of her breath and the eagerness of her lips and her deep panting against my neck as the consummation of the act for which she had come, and for which she had assumed the disguise of Beatrice, came nearer. All the others had been fools, she had said, and I can make you mad with love for me. It was true.

Yet I struggled against the mail-strength of her wrists as she held me down on the couch. My fingers were tearing at the yellow hair, pulling her head backwards. It made no difference. Nothing was now going to stop her. Already a stream of blood was coming, hot and living, from the side of my neck and her lips were pressing to fix themselves upon the desired food. She was supernatural in her thirst. I knew now what Pauline felt; I knew the longing she must have had to surrender, to give myself, my body, my life to this fearful thing. I began to love and to want this evil love.

What moment of sanity allowed me to twist sideways I do not know. With my one free hand I searched for the protector I had put ready. I could feel it on the wall and I tore down the mirror. My twisting freed me long enough to turn again to the panting, eager thing on the couch and to hold the mirror, with trembling hands, before its face.

'Look,' I cried, daring myself, too, to look on the face of Elaine, the sharp, elongated face, the teeth and the mane-like hair already turning black. She raised her eyes at my command, her whole body pulsing with desire to throw herself on me again. But now the mirror was between us, its simple safety like a shield before me. The mirror which no vampire can withstand because they see no image in it.

With a terrified shriek like the splitting noise of owls in the night, she flung her claws of hands before her face and went. Only a tinkling of glass on the path outside the house, and the few strands of black hair caught on a nail, showed which way she had gone. With her went the siren-calling music and the mist.

I stopped the bleeding from my neck and went outside. I walked about the whole building, carrying the mirror before me as a guard. And the night was still again. Only I could not get out of my mind the picture of Elaine when I confronted her with the mirror, the animal lust on her face, the red glow of her eyes and my wet blood on her feline lips. I knew I had been lucky.

***

I must be quick if I was to save Pauline. Now that Elaine had revealed herself fully to me I was within the full orbit of her power and whatever enchantment she used to draw Pauline to her would fall on me, too. It was not enough to have defeated her once.

When her music began again I was hiding in a spinney to the left of that grove of fir trees on the other side of the lake. I first heard the soft, calling, voice coming across the meadows. The calling began so softly that, perhaps, I only became aware of it when the wood pigeon high in the trees ceased its cooing. But, from the moment I did hear it, eddying over the atmosphere like the circles from a stone thrown into a pool, it grew stronger until the whole of Landred was suffused by its subtle influence. I doubt if anyone, certainly someone like Pauline who did not know what it meant, could have resisted its call, so soft, so tender and loving and yet so powerful was it. And the horror was that, for all my escape in the cottage, I was still half suborned by her music. I wanted to leave the ditch of dry leaves and go to the castle window from which the enchantment was coming and, even then, give my blood to Elaine that she might continue to live. To do so, then, seemed a most desirable thing. My whole body ached to be one with her's.

Pauline, who did not know what was required of her, would be aware only that she must go to Elaine at once. There had never been any question of her disobeying the enchantment and, even when she was in France, Elaine (who needed her badly to continue to live) was able to reach her. I forced myself to remain where I was, repeating to myself that in this battle between the living and the dead, it was still necessary to use all my intelligence.

And then the white-clad figure of Pauline came into sight. The time had come to act, to leave my bed of dried leaves, to come to an end of these temptations and enchantments. I ran out across the grass to the great door of the castle ruin through which, only a moment before, Pauline had passed. I flung myself against it and pulled at the iron handle. The massive oak slab did not move. Elaine had locked it as soon as she was certain of Pauline.

Sixty feet above me spun out the arc of yellow light from the open windows of her room. There was nothing to do but to climb. I could see the thick, gnarled, twisting ivy above me. I leapt and clung to it and pulled myself up on to the rotting roof. I heaved myself into the shelter of a wall. I went on, in the dusklight, my hands grimed with brick dust and across the back of my left hand a gash where I had caught it, in my haste, against the sharp angle of a piece of iron.

I looked over into the meadows a long way below and saw that I was standing at the corner of the ruined tower and that the ivy, going up the face of the wall, here turned and began to go upward to her room. Above the stillness of approaching night one sound began to drown all others. I knew that sound, it had filled my cottage only a little while ago. Without hesitation I flung myself over the side of the wall and, clinging to the ivy, began to pull myself towards the lighted window. I had only one thought. I must get through that window before Elaine had time to destroy her victim, for this time she needed to be surfeited with blood, so long had she been without. I dragged my arms over the ledge and looked in.

Before me, on a large white divan, Pauline was lying, quite naked, her eyes staring with incredible love into Elaine's. I saw Elaine crouch over the naked body of

Pauline, caressing her breasts, purring with pleasure at the thought of what was to follow, her claw-like hands beginning to caress the neck of her victim. The girl allowed Elaine to do what she liked, and it was evident that she was in some kind of trance. And then, as I watched, Elaine lowered her head and began to caress Pauline's neck with her lips.

I don't know what I did to distract her attention. Perhaps my foot slipped and made a noise searching for a new foothold

The tension on my arms was intolerable. Suddenly Elaine looked up from her prey and our eyes met.

The face I saw while we stared at each other there was the face of some fierce batlike creature, ugly, monstrous. Her black hair was streaming down the cheeks of that face, a black tiger's mane. The utter transformation of her features was horrible, transfixed by hate and the knowledge we both shared that, at all costs, she must have Pauline's blood, the food this dead-alive thing needed. Without it she must die, without it she, who came from the ancient vaults of the church on the Hedingham estate and was, perhaps, the incarnation of all the Hedinghams who ever lived here, must return to the dark forever. In that moment, afraid of her as I was, I pitied her her endless sojourn on earth; I pitied her who, so beautiful when living on Pauline's blood, could now look so loathsome.

Those eyes, closer together than usual, glowed with that red fire I had already seen in my own house. From the mouth which had once seemed so seductive to me, two long, sharp, teeth protruded, teeth with which she would pierce the neck of the girl lying, inert, beneath her; teeth which had stabbed me, too. How many times had she drawn the life-blood from Pauline; from others down the centuries?

I knew that, in a second, she would be upon me to kill me. I clung to the ivy when she sprang. The great catlike animal was across the stone-flagged floor of that castle room with one enormous spring. I had not realised that it was possible for her to take so potent a disguise, but when she took a second spring and rose into the air to fall on me with her fearful claws, I pulled myself downwards below the coping of the window and pressed my body into the brickwork and felt the arm of ivy tear into my ribs. With the spread of its spring the animal, which was Elaine, unable to check itself when I disappeared, went over my head into the night. The leaves of the ivy rustled as if a wind had got into them.

With a sob I dragged my body into the room and ran to Pauline.

***

'Are you sure you want to come with me?' I asked.

'Yes, of course.' Beatrice said. 'But, Charles, do you mean that Elaine didn't really exist at all?'

'Oh, she existed all right. She existed all the time she was able to get what she needed from others. But mostly from Pauline who is in direct descent. Pauline was a gift to her.'

'But, Charles, it's too awful. It will upset Pauline for the rest of her life, if she realises...'

'I don't think she does. Actually, I think, she supposes that Elaine has gone away for good. In any case Elaine meant this to be the last time. She intended to kill Pauline. There was no other way. She herself was very weak. Then she, too, would have gone. To a new victim.'

'Gone? Where?'

'Oh, somewhere near at hand, that's obvious because she needed to return here every night. But she knew she must go from Landred as soon as she saw me and heard what I said at Pauline's birthday party. If she could not kill me, and she tried twice, then she had no choice but to leave. She had learned, as these creatures always do, a very subtle magic, and she could assume any shape she wished.'

'But, Charles, I didn't know.' Beatrice was taken aback. 'She tried to kill you twice?'

'Yes. But now I think we ought to get across to the church. Your man will have got the door of the vault open. Are you still sure you want to come? What I have to do won't be pleasant.'

'I still don't understand,' she said. 'When this thing which was Elaine sprang from the divan and so fell to its death, you say nothing was to be found on the ground below?'

'Nothing but the marks of claws. Not even a drop of blood.'

'Why? And where is Elaine now? I'm sure she was alive.'

'Alive, indeed, she was, my dear. Alive with the blood she took so frequently from your daughter.'

'How ghastly! Thank God you got there in time.'

'Yes,' I said. 'But the real saviour is you. For, thank God

in my turn, when her subtle enchantments began last evening while I watched the castle ruin, I remembered you. Forgive my saying this at such a moment. I remembered I loved you.'

Beatrice stopped. We were halfway down the avenue of yews leading to the church door. 'Charles,' she said, 'dear Charles.' In the darkened sunlight of the age-old trees her golden hair was very lovely.

When we reached the nave and saw the stone turned to one side and the steps going down into the vault, the clock in the tower struck twelve. Tom, Beatrice's man-of-all-work, may have had a shrewd idea of our errand. At all events he suggested to his mistress that she stay in the church while he and I went into the vault alone. But Beatrice persisted and Tom, lifting the lantern, led the way down the steps. The vault was full and had not been opened for years. On each side of a central aisle were racks of coffins, Beatrice's ancestors.

There was no sound but our breathing when I held the light in my hands and let it fall on the plate of one of the further-in coffins. ELAINE HEDINGHAM, I read, DIED 1459. AGED TWENTY-EIGHT. Gently I lifted the well-preserved wooden lid and looked on the fair face of Elaine as I had seen her the night of Pauline's birthday party.

She was beautiful with a magical beauty, her black hair falling about her shroud and her hands, in living flesh, closed on her breast. Beatrice gave a little scream and I could feel her body close to me for protection. I knew that she was looking as if into a mirror and seeing, in the lovely face below her, her own reflection. I knew what I had to do, but so beautiful was Elaine that my heart sank in me. Could she but have risen up before us in all her loveliness, I believe my courage would have deserted me. And then I remembered the thing she had become the night before; I remembered the weak, pitifully weak girl Pauline had become at the hands of this beautiful woman lying below me now.

With a pity I have never known since, I took the stake from Tom's hands and struck. While we watched the blood spurted over her limbs. It was a terrible moment and, perhaps, our agony was as great as her's. Yet, while we could not take our eyes from the coffin, the body of the woman we had known as Elaine, which once, centuries ago, had been Elaine Hedingham walking and talking in the groves and gardens of Landred, gave a little sigh. I have since convinced myself that what I did that day was what she would have had me do, and that, at last, she was happy. The fair face and body of the woman whose blood still ran thinly in Beatrice's veins turned to dust and only the skull remained covered with midnight black hair. And it was as if the sun came into that dark, cold place. Even the other coffins glowed with a faint light. Yet her loveliness haunts me still.

SELECT BIBLIOGRAPHY

Rollo Ahmed, *The Black Art* 1936
Basil Copper *The Vampire in Legend, Tact and Art* 1973
Richard Cavendish *The Black Arts* 1967
James Dickie *The Undead* 1971
Douglas Drake *Horrors* 1967
Robert Eisler *Man Into Wolf* 1951
Douglas Hill and Pat Williams *The Supernatural* 1965
Harry Ludlam *A Biography of Dracula* 1962
Anthony Masters *The Natural History of the Vampire* 1972
Raymond T *In Search of Dracula* 1973
McNally and Radu Florescu *Dracula* 1974
William Seabrook *Witchcraft* 1941
Montague Summers *The Vampire: His Kith and Kin* 1928; *The Vampire in Europe* 1929
Roger Vadim *The Vampire* 1963
Ornella Volta *The Vampire* 1965

A scene from *Vampire Circus* (1974) a Hammer Film Production for The Rank Organisation. The gypsy woman (Adrienne Corri) forces Gerta (Elizabeth Seal) backwards over the body of Count Mitterhouse (Robert Tayman) for Emil (Anthony Corlan) to sink his vampire fangs into her neck.

ABOUT THE AUTHOR

Peter Underwood

Peter Underwood was President of
the Ghost Club (founded 1862) from
1960-1993 and probably heard more
first-hand ghost stories than any man
alive. He was a long-standing member of The Society of Psychical Research, Vice-President of the Unitarian Society for Psychical Studies, a
member of The Folklore Society, The Dracula Society
and the Research Committee of the Psychic Research
Organization, he wrote extensively, and was a seasoned
lecturer and broadcaster. He took part in the first official investigation into a haunting; sat with physical
and mental mediums and conducted investigations at
seances. He was present at exorcisms, experiments at
dowsing, precognition, clairvoyance, hypnotism, regression; he conducted world-wide tests in telepathy
and extra-sensory perception, and personally investigated scores of haunted houses across the country. He
possessed comprehensive files of alleged hauntings in
every county of the British Isles and many foreign
countries, and his knowledge and experience resulted
in his being consulted on psychic and occult matters

by the BBC and ITV. His many books include the first two comprehensive gazetteers of ghosts and hauntings in England, Scotland and Ireland and two books that deal with twenty different occult subjects. Highlights from his published work include 'Nights in Haunted Houses' (1993), which collects together the results of group investigations, 'The Ghosts of Borley' (1973), his classic account of the history of 'the most haunted house in England', 'Hauntings' (1977), which re-examines ten classic cases of haunting in the light of modern knowledge, 'No Common Task' (1983), which reflects back upon his life as a 'ghost hunter', and 'The Ghost Hunter's Guide' (1986), which gives the reader all the advice necessary to become one. Born at Letchworth Garden City in Hertfordshire, he lived for many years in a small village in Hampshire.

BOOKS BY THIS AUTHOR

The Ghosts Of Borley: Annals Of The Haunted Rectory

'The Ghosts of Borley' (1973) was the first complete record of the unique Borley Rectory hauntings, detailing all the evidence known about this notorious haunted house from the early days of the Rev. H. D. E. Bull who built Borley Rectory in 1863, through the incumbencies of the Rev. Harry Bull, the Rev. Guy Eric Smith and the Rev. Lionel Foyster, to the investigations by Harry Price and other members of the Society for Psychical Research (SPR).

The Ghost Hunters: Who They Are And What They Do

A leading psychical researcher takes an in-depth look at ghost hunters, both past and present. Who are these intrepid explorers of the unknown? How do they probe and examine the realms of the seemingly inexplicable? What are their conclusions? In fascinating detail, Peter Underwood profiles the lives and adventures of some of the most famous names in psychical investigation.

The Ghost Hunter's Guide

What are the qualities which make an ideal ghost hunter? You need to be part detective, part investigative reporter, a scientist, with a measure of the psychologist thrown in...

In this book, which is the first real guide to the hunting of ghosts, Peter Underwood manages to cover just about every aspect of this intriguing and mystifying subject.

Nights In Haunted Houses

For over thirty years, in his position as President and Chief Investigator of the Ghost Club of Great Britain, Peter Underwood was actively involved in undertaking night vigils and carrying out research into ghosts and paranormal activity in controlled, scientific conditions.

Into The Occult

Despite all the answers that conventional science can provide to the earth's mysteries, there remain certain phenomena for which no explanation can yet be found outside the occult. For this reason exploration of the occult and paranormal provides endless fascination.

Here is a survey of all the different aspects of this complex and intriguing subject, including an entire chapter on the relationship between sex and psychic phenom-

ena, a subject on which, until recently, there has been an unwillingness to talk.

Deeper Into The Occult

'In an age when voodoo dancers have appeared in London, when Robert Williams, chief psychologist at Kansas State Industrial Reformatory admits to being a practising war-lock; when moon-astronaut Edgar Mitchell conducts extra sensory experiments in space; when the course of a £1,000,000 road is altered to save a 'fairy tree'; when a ghost is officially registered on a census form; when Americans can 'dial-a-horoscope' for a twenty-four hour prophesy; and when the complete skeleton of a cyclops is unearthed by archaeologists — is it surprising that there is a growing interest in the occult, for research in many fields simply proves that things are not what they seem?'

The Complete Book Of Dowsing And Divining

This comprehensive volume on dowsing and divining - from the twig and the pendulum to motorscopes and bare hands - traces the story of these fascinating and enigmatic phenomena from its origins in the world of fairy tales and mythology to recent theories that the enigma can be explained in terms of present-day psychology.

Peter Underwood's Guide To Ghosts & Haunted Places

Based on 50 years' expert study and investigation, this collection of cases from the files of Peter Underwood - an acknowledged expert and experienced investigator of haunted houses - represents a unique exploration of the world of ghosts, apparitions and psychic phenomena. If you want to satisfy your curiosity about the subject or simply enjoy a riveting read, this guide is for you.

Jack The Ripper: One Hundred Years Of Mystery

Jack the Ripper still causes a shudder, synonymous as it is with violent murder and mutilation. But also of mystery and speculation - for the gruesome series of killings in London's East End in that horrific Autumn of 1888 have never been finally solved.

Ghosts Of Hampshire And The Isle Of Wight

Peter Underwood, an acknowledged expert and experienced investigator of haunted houses, presents a selection of hauntings throughout Hampshire and the Isle of Wight. A formidable collection of ghoulies and things that go bump in the night.

This edition includes a foreword by author Alan Williams, as well as an interview Williams conducted with Underwood in 1997.

Dictionary Of The Supernatural

An A to Z of Hauntings, Possession, Witchcraft, Demon-

ology and Other Occult Phenomena...

The entries cover all known (and some very little known) organisations, individuals, periodicals, terms of reference, and significant cases, events and incidents relevant to the subject. Under each entry there are notes on other appropriate books and further reading.

No Common Task: The Autobiography Of A Ghost-Hunter

This is the autobiography of a man who has spent thirty-five years of his life covering scientific psychical research, with detailed investigations into all kinds of manifestation that might be supernatural or paranormal in origin, including spiritualism, ESP, telepathy, hauntings and other occult phenomena. Many of the true experiences from the author's casebook are published here for the first time.

Death In Hollywood

The Hollywood way of life has long been a potent mix of scandal, secrecy and sensation: exactly like the Hollywood way of death...

In this unique study, Peter Underwood charts the lives, loves and deaths of thirty of Tinseltown's most glittering stars. Many deaths were sad or senseless; some were tragic; others were the revenge of old age, while a few were the revenge of something altogether more sinister...

Exorcism!

Throughout history, the practice of exorcism has been used for the purpose of driving out evil spirits and demons though to possess human beings and the places they inhabit. But there are more startling instances where exorcism has been used: to cure a trawler that seemed to be cursed; to expel demons from Bram Stoker's black 'vampire' dog' even to rid Loch Ness and the Bermuda Triangle of their evil ambience. Peter Underwood explores this frightening ritual in relation to witches, vampires and animals, while his far-flung researches have unearthed dramatic cases in Morocco, Egypt, South Africa and the United States, as well as the British Isles.

This Haunted Isle

Peter Underwood has personally visited the historic buildings and sites of Britain, and here presents a wealth of intriguing legends and new stories of ghostly encounters from more than a hundred such throughout the United Kingdom.
From Abbey House in Cambridge to Zennor in Cornwall, this is an A to Z of the haunted houses of Britain. At Bramshill in Hampshire — now a police training college — there have been so many sightings that even sceptical police officers have had to admit that the place is haunted. Beautiful Leeds Castle in Kent has a large, phantom black dog; there is an Elizabethan gentleman (seen by a Canon of the Church of England!) at Croft Castle; a Pink Lady at Coughton Court; a pran-

cing ghost jester at Gawsworth; a spectre in green velvet at Hoghton Tower; six ghosts at East Riddlesden Hall; a headless apparition at Westwood Manor; and then there are some little-known ghosts in Windsor Castle, Hampton Court Palace and the Tower of London, and the strange ghosts of Chingle Hall, perhaps the most haunted house in England.

Hauntings: New Light On The Greatest True Ghost Stories Of The World

In this fascinating account of the best-attested cases of haunting - Hampton Court, the demon drummer of Bedworth, the Wesley ghost, Glamis, Borley Rectory and many others - Britain's foremost ghost-hunter has brought to light a wealth of valuable new evidence. Using the results of his many years of research and personal investigation into ghosts and hauntings, and providing detailed plans and original photographs, Peter Underwood puts forward some exciting and startling theories which will radically change our ideas about these hauntings.

Karloff: The Life Of Boris Karloff

Boris Karloff was the most famous of all horror actors. His memorable portrayal of the Frankenstein monster added a new word to English dictionaries.

Ghosts Of Kent

The first expert exploration of the haunted houses and authentic ghosts of Kent by the [former] President of

the Ghost Club, Peter Underwood.

Ghosts Of North West England

The ghostly little monk of Foulridge and the giant apparition from Heaton Norris are just two of the denizens of the North-West you might not care to meet on a dark, stormy evening. But for those intrepid souls whose hearts quicken at the thought of eerie footsteps and muffled groans Peter Underwood has assembled an impressive collection of traditional legends.

Queen Victoria's Other World

There have been many books about Queen Victoria but there has never been one that has explored her 'other world' - the world of the strange and unusual, the world of death and her fascination for it, and the world of the unseen and the paranormal that she could never resist.

Made in United States
Troutdale, OR
05/06/2024